Complete Poems; Edited With Memorial-Introd. and Notes by Alexander B. Grosart

Robert Herrick, Alexander Balloch Grosart

Copyright © BiblioLife, LLC

This book represents a historical reproduction of a work originally published before 1923 that is part of a unique project which provides opportunities for readers, educators and researchers by bringing hard-to-find original publications back into print at reasonable prices. Because this and other works are culturally important, we have made them available as part of our commitment to protecting, preserving and promoting the world's literature. These books are in the "public domain" and were digitized and made available in cooperation with libraries, archives, and open source initiatives around the world dedicated to this important mission.

We believe that when we undertake the difficult task of re-creating these works as attractive, readable and affordable books, we further the goal of sharing these works with a global audience, and preserving a vanishing wealth of human knowledge.

Many historical books were originally published in small fonts, which can make them very difficult to read. Accordingly, in order to improve the reading experience of these books, we have created "enlarged print" versions of our books. Because of font size variation in the original books, some of these may not technically qualify as "large print" books, as that term is generally defined; however, we believe these versions provide an overall improved reading experience for many.

Early English Poets.

ROBERT HERRICK.

Early English Poets.

THE
COMPLETE POEMS
OF
ROBERT HERRICK.

EDITED,

WITH

Memorial-Introduction and Notes,

BY THE

REV. ALEXANDER B. GROSART.

IN THREE VOLUMES.—VOL. III.

London:
CHATTO AND WINDUS, PICCADILLY.
1876.

PR
3510
A5G76
18??
v.3

1534
———
16/9/91

Contents.

	PAGE
HESPERIDES :—	
The showre of Blossomes	1
Upon Spenke	1
A Defence for Women	2
Upon Lulls	2
Slavery	2
Charmes	2
Another	3
Another to bring in the Witch	3
Another Charme for Stables	3
Ceremonies for Candlemasse Eve	4
The Ceremonies for Candlemasse day	5
Upon Candlemasse day	6
Surfeits	6
Upon Nis	6
To Biancha, to blesse him	6
Julia's Churching, or Purification	7
To his Book	8
Teares	8
To his friend to avoid contention of words	8
Truth	9
Upon Prickles. Epig.	9
The Eyes before the Eares	9
Want	9

CONTENTS.

	PAGE
HESPERIDES *(continued)*	
To a Friend	9
Upon M. William Lawes, the rare Musitian	10
A Song upon Silvia	10
The Hony-combe	11
Vpon Ben. Johnson	11
An Ode for him	11
Upon a Virgin	12
Blame	13
A request to the Graces	13
Upon himselfe	13
Multitude	14
Feare	14
To M. Kellam	14
Happinesse to hospitalitie, or a hearty to good house-keeping	15
Cunctation in correction	16
Present Government grievous	16
Rest Refreshes	16
Revenge	17
The first marrs or makes	17
Beginning, difficult	17
Faith four-square	17
The present time best pleaseth	18
Cloathes, are conspirators	18
Cruelty	18
Faire after foule	18
Hunger	18
Bad wages for good service	18
The End	19

CONTENTS.

	PAGE
HESPERIDES *(continued)*	
The Bondman	19
Choose for the best	19
To Silvia	19
Faire shewes deceive	20
His wish	20
Upon Julia's washing her self in the river	20
A Meane in our Meanes	21
Upon Clunn	21
Upon Cupid	21
Vpon Blisse	22
Vpon Burr	22
Vpon Megg	23
An Hymne to Love	23
To his honoured and most ingenious friend, Mr. Charles Cotton	24
Women uselesse	25
Love is a sirrup	25
Leven	26
Repletion	26
On Himselfe	26
No Man without Money	26
On Himselfe	26
To M. Leonard Willan his peculiar friend	27
To his worthy Friend M. John Hall, Student of Grayes-Inne	27
To Julia	28
To the most comely and proper M. Elizabeth Finch	28
Upon Ralph	29

CONTENTS.

HESPERIDES (continued)   PAGE
To his Booke 29
To the King, upon his welcome to Hampton-
    Court 30
Ultimus Heroum : or, To the most Learned, and
    to the right Honourable, Henry, Marquesse
    of Dorchester 31
To his Muse, another to the same . . . 31
Upon Vineger 32
Upon Mudge 32
To his learned Friend M. Jo. Harmar, Phisitian
    to the Colledge of Westminster . . . 32
Upon his Spaniell Tracie 33
The Deluge 33
Upon Lupes 34
Raggs 34
Strength to support Soveraignty . . . 34
Upon Tubbs 34
Crutches 35
To Julia 36
Upon Case 36
To Perenna 37
To his Sister in Law, M. Susanna Herrick . . 37
Upon the Lady Crew 37
On Tomasin Parsons 38
Ceremony upon Candlemas Eve 38
Suspicion makes secure 38
Upon Spokes 38
To his Kinsman, M. Tho: Herrick, who desired
    to be in his Book 39

CONTENTS.

	PAGE
HESPERIDES *(continued)*	
A Bucolick betwixt Two : Lacon and Thyrsis	39
Upon Sapho	41
Upon Faunus	41
The Quintell.	41
A Bachanalian Verse	42
Care a good keeper	42
Rules for our reach	42
To Biancha	43
To the handsome Mistresse Grace Potter	43
Anacreontike	43
More modest, more manly	45
Not to covet much where little is the charge	45
Anacreontick Verse	45
Upon Pennie	45
Patience in Princes	46
Feare gets force	46
Parcell-gil't-Poetry	46
Upon Love, by way of question and answer	46
To the Lord Hopton, on his fight in Cornwall	47
His Grange	47
Leprosie in houses	48
Good Manners at meat	48
Anthea's Retractation	49
Comforts in Crosses	49
Seeke and finde	49
Rest	49
Leprosie in Cloathes	50
Upon Buggins	50
Great Maladies, long Medicines	50

CONTENTS.

HESPERIDES (*continued*)

	PAGE
His Answer to a friend	50
The Begger	51
Bastards	51
His change	51
The Vision	52
A Vow to Venus	52
On his Booke	53
A Sonnet of Perilla	53
Bad may be better	53
Posting to Printing	53
Rapine brings Ruine	53
Comfort to a youth that had lost his Love	54
Upon Boreman. Epig.	55
Saint Distaff's day, or the morrow after Twelfth day	55
Sufferance	56
His teares to Thamasis	56
Pardons	57
Peace not Permanent	57
Truth and Errour	58
Things mortall, still mutable	58
Studies to be supported	58
Wit punisht, prospers most	58
Twelfe night, or King and Queene	58
His desire	60
Caution in Councell	60
Moderation	60
Advice the best actor	60
Conformity is comely	61
Lawes	61

CONTENTS.

	PAGE
HESPERIDES *(continued)*	
The meane	61
Like loves his like	61
His Hope or sheat-Anchor	61
Comfort in Calamity	62
Twilight	62
False Mourning	62
The will makes the work, or consent makes the Cure	62
Diet	62
Smart	63
The Tinkers Song	63
His Comfort	64
Sincerity	64
To Anthea	64
Nor buying or selling	64
To his peculiar friend M. Jo: Wicks	65
The more mighty, the more mercifull	65
After Autumne, Winter	66
A good death	66
Recompence	66
On Fortune	66
To Sir George Parrie, Doctor of the Civill Law	66
Charmes	67
Another	67
Another	68
Upon Gorgonius	68
Gentlenesse	68
A Dialogue betwixt himselfe and Mistresse Eliza: Wheeler, under the name of Amarillis	69

	PAGE
HESPERIDES *(continued)*	
To Julia	70
To Roses in Julia's Bosome	70
To the honoured Master Endimion Porter	70
Speake in season	71
Obedience	71
Another on the same	71
Of Love	71
Upon Trap	72
Upon Grubs	72
Upon Dol	72
Upon Hog	72
The School or Perl of Putney, the Mistress of all singular manners, Mistresse Portman	73
To Perenna	74
On himselfe	74
On Love	74
Another on Love	75
Upon Gut	75
Upon Chub	75
Pleasures Pernicious	75
On himself	75
To M. Laurence Swetnaham	76
His Covenant or Protestation to Julia	76
On himselfe	77
To the most accomplisht Gentleman Master Michael Oulsworth	77
To his Girles who would have him sportfull	78
Truth and falsehood	78
His last request to Julia	78

CONTENTS. xiii.

PAGE

HESPERIDES *(continued)*

On himselfe	79
Upon Kings	79
To his Girles	79
Upon Spur	79
To his Brother Nicolas Herrick	80
The Voice and Violl	81
Warre	81
A King and no King	81
Plots not still prosperous	81
Flatterie	82
Upon Rumpe	82
Upon Shopter	82
Upon Deb	82
Excesse	82
Upon Croot	82
The Soul is the salt	83
Upon Flood, or a thankfull man	83
Upon Pimpe	83
Upon Luske	83
Foolishnesse	83
Upon Rush	84
Abstinence	84
No danger to men desperate	84
Sauce for sorrowes	84
To Cupid	84
Distrust	85
The Hagg	85
The mount of the Muses	86
On Himselfe	86

CONTENTS.

	PAGE
HESPERIDES *(continued)*	
To his Booke	86
The end of his worke	87
To Crowne it	87
On Himselfe	87
The pillar of Fame	88
GOLDEN APPLES.	
The Discription of a Woman	91
Mr. Hericke his Daughters Dowrye	96
Mr. Robert Hericke his Farwell vnto Poetrie	101
A Charroll presented to Dr. Williams, Bp. of Lincolne, as a Newyears Guift	106
Song. His Mistris to him at his Farwell	108
Vpon Parting	109
Upon Master Fletchers Incomparable Playes	109
The New Charon, upon the Death of Henry Lord Hastings	110
Epitaph on the Tomb of Sir Edward Giles & his wife in the South Aisle of Dean Prior Church, Devon	113
NOBLE NUMBERS.	
His Confession	119
His Prayer for Absolution	119
To finde God	120
What God is	121
Upon God	121
Mercy and Love	121
Gods Anger without Affection	121
God not to be comprehended	122
Gods part	122

CONTENTS.

	PAGE
NOBLE NUMBERS *(continued)*	
Affliction	122
Three fatall Sisters	122
Silence	122
Mirth	123
Loading and unloading	123
Gods Mercy	123
Prayers must have Poise	123
To God: an Anthem, sung in the Chappell at White-Hall, before the King	124
Upon God	124
Calling, and correcting	124
No Escaping the scourging	124
The Rod	125
God has a twofold part	125
God is One	125
Persecutions profitable	125
To God	125
Whips	126
Gods Providence	126
Temptation	126
His Ejaculation to God	126
Gods gifts not soone granted	127
Persecutions purifie	127
Pardon	127
An Ode of the Birth of our Saviour	128
Lip-labour	129
The Heart	129
Eare-rings	130
Sin seen	130

CONTENTS.

	PAGE
NOBLE NUMBERS *(continued)*	
Upon Time	130
His Petition	131
To God	131
His Letanie, to the Holy Spirit	132
Thanksgiving	134
Cock-crow	134
All Things run well for the Righteous	135
Paine ends in Pleasure	135
To God	135
A Thanksgiving to God, for His House	135
To God	138
Another, to God	138
None truly happy here	139
To his ever-loving God	139
Another	140
To Death	140
Neutrality loathsome	141
Welcome what comes	141
To his angrie God	141
Patience, or Comforts in Crosses	142
Eternitie	142
To his Saviour, a Child; a Present, by a child	143
The New-yeeres Gift	144
To God	144
God, and the King	144
Gods mirth, Mans mourning	145
Honours are hindrances	145
The Parasceve, or Preparation	145
To God	146

CONTENTS.

	PAGE
NOBLE NUMBERS (*continued*)	
A will to be working	146
Christs part	146
Riches and Poverty	146
Sobriety in Search	147
Almes	147
To his Conscience	147
To his Saviour	148
To God	148
His Dreame	148
Gods Bounty	149
To his sweet Saviour	149
His Creed	150
Temptations	151
The Lamp	151
Sorrowes	151
Penitencie	151
The Dirge of Jephthahs Daughter : sung by the Virgins	151
To God, on his sicknesse	155
Sins loath'd, and yet lov'd	156
Sin	156
Upon God	156
Faith	156
Humility	156
Teares	157
Sin and Strife	157
An Ode, or Psalme, to God	157
Graces for Children	158
God to be first serv'd	158

CONTENTS.

	PAGE
NOBLE NUMBERS *(continued)*	
Another Grace for a Child	158
A Christmas Caroll, sung to the King in the Presence at White-Hall	159
The New-yeeres Gift, or Circumcisions Song, sung to the King in the Presence at White-Hall	161
Another New-yeeres Gift, or Song for the Circumcision	162
Gods Pardon	164
Sin	164
Evill	164
The Star-Song: a Caroll to the King; sung at White-Hall	165
To God	166
To his deere God	166
To God, his good will	167
On Heaven	168
The Summe, and the Satisfaction	168
Good men afflicted most	169
Good Christians	170
The Will the cause of Woe	170
To Heaven	170
The Recompence	170
To God	171
To God	171
His wish to God	172
Satan	172
Hell	173
The way	173

CONTENTS.   xix.

	PAGE
NOBLE NUMBERS (*continued*)	
Great grief, great glory	173
Hell	173
The Bell-man	174
The goodnesse of his God	174
The Widdowes teares: or, Dirge of Dorcas	175
To God, in time of plundering	179
To his Saviour. The New-yeers gift	179
Doomes-Day	180
The Poores Portion	180
The White Island: or place of the Blest	180
To Christ	182
To God	182
Free Welcome	182
Gods Grace	182
Coming to Christ	183
Correction	183
Gods Bounty	183
Knowledge	183
Salutation	183
Lasciviousnesse	184
Teares	184
Gods Blessing	184
God, and Lord	184
The Judgment-Day	184
Angells	185
Long life	185
Teares	185
Manna	185
Reverence	185

CONTENTS.

NOBLE NUMBERS (*continued*)

	PAGE
Mercy	186
Wages	186
Temptation	186
Gods hands	186
Labour	186
Mora Sponsi, the stay of the Bridegroome	187
Roaring	187
The Eucharist	187
Sin severely punisht	187
Montes Scripturarum, the Mounts of the Scriptures	187
Prayer	188
Christs sadnesse	188
God heares us	188
God	188
Clouds	189
Comforts in contentions	189
Heaven	189
God	189
His Power	189
Christs words on the Crosse, My God, My God	189
Jehovah	190
Confusion of face	190
Another	190
Beggars	190
Good, and bad	191
Sin	191
Martha, Martha	191
Youth, and Age	191

	PAGE
NOBLE NUMBERS *(continued)*	
Gods Power	191
Paradise	191
Observation	192
The Asse	192
Observation	192
Tapers	193
Christs Birth	193
The Virgin Mary	193
Another	194
God	194
Another of God	194
Another	194
Gods presence	194
Gods Dwelling	195
The Virgin Mary	195
To God	196
Upon Woman and Mary	196
North and South	196
Sabbaths	197
The Fast, or Lent	197
Sin	197
God	197
This, and the next World	198
Ease	198
Beginnings and Endings	198
Temporall Goods	198
Hell fire	199
Abels Bloud	199
Another	199

NOBLE NUMBERS (continued)

	PAGE
A Position in the Hebrew Divinity	199
Penitence	200
God's presence	200
The Resurrection possible, and probable	200
Christs Suffering	200
Sinners	201
Temptations	201
Pittie, and punishment	201
Gods price, and mans price	201
Christs Action	201
Predestination	202
Another	202
Sin	202
Another	202
Another	203
Prescience	203
Christ	203
Christs Incarnation	203
Heaven	203
Gods keyes	204
Sin	204
Almes	204
Hell fire	204
To keep a true Lent	204
No time in Eternitie	206
His Meditation upon Death	206
Cloaths for Continuance	207
To God	208
The Soule	208

CONTENTS.

	PAGE
NOBLE NUMBERS (continued)	
The Judgement-day	209
Sufferings	209
Paine and pleasure	209
Gods presence	209
Another	209
The poore mans part	210
The right hand	210
The Staffe and Rod	210
God sparing in scourging	210
Confession	210
Gods descent	211
No coming to God without Christ	211
Another, to God	211
The Resurrection	212
Coheires	212
The number of two	212
Hardning of hearts	212
The Rose	213
Gods time must end our trouble	213
Baptisme	213
Gold and Frankincense	213
To God	214
The chewing the Cud	214
Christs twofold coming	214
To God, his gift	215
Gods Anger	215
Gods Commands	215
To God	215
To God	216

	PAGE
NOBLE NUMBERS *(continued)*	
Good Friday: Rex Tragicus, or Christ going to His Crosse	216
His words to Christ, going to the Crosse	218
Another, to his Saviour	218
His Saviours words, going to the Crosse	219
His Anthem, to Christ on the Crosse	220
This Crosse-Tree here	221
To his Saviours Sepulcher: his Devotion	222
His Offering, with the rest, at the Sepulcher	223
His coming to the Sepulcher	223
Of all the good things whatsoe're we do	224
INDEX OF FIRST LINES	227
GLOSSARIAL INDEX	283
INDEX OF NAMES	305

HESPERIDES.

The showre of Blossomes.

OVE in a showre of Blossomes came
Down, and halfe drown'd me with the same
The Blooms that fell were white and red;
But with such sweets comminglèd,
As whether (this) I cannot tell
My sight was pleas'd more, or my smell:
But true it was, as I rowl'd there,
Without a thought of hurt, or feare;
Love turn'd himselfe into a Bee,
And with his Javelin wounded me:
From which mishap this use I make,
Where most sweets are, there lyes a Snake:
Kisses and Favours are sweet things;
But Those have thorns, and These have stings.

Upon Spenke.

SPENKE has a strong breath, yet short Prayers
      saith:
Not out-of want of breath, but want of faith.

A Defence for Women.

NAUGHT are all Women : I say no,
　　Since for one Bad, one Good I know :
For *Clytemnestra* most unkind,
Loving *Alcestis* there we find :
For one *Medea* that was bad,
A good *Penelope* was had :
For wanton *Lais*, then we have
Chaste *Lucrece*, or a wife as grave :
And thus through Woman-kind we see
A Good and Bad.　*Sirs credit me.*

Upon Lulls.

LULLS swears he is all heart ; but you'l suppose
　　By his *Probossis* that he is all nose.

Slavery.

'TIS liberty to serve one Lord ; but he
　　Who many serves, serves base servility.[1]

Charmes.

BRING the holy crust of Bread,
　　Lay it underneath the head ;

---

[1] Cf. the Page's argument that servants are less servants than their masters, in Massinger's Unnatural Combat : Act iii. sc. 2.

    'Tis a certain Charm to keep
    Hags away, while Children sleep.

Another.

LET the superstitious wife
    Neer the child's heart lay a knife:
Point be up, and Haft be downe;
(While she gossips in the towne)
This 'mongst other mystick charms
Keeps the sleeping child from harms.[2]

Another to bring in the Witch.

TO house[3] the Hag, you must doe this;
    Commix with Meale a little Pisse
Of him bewitcht: then forthwith make
A little Wafer or a Cake:
And this rawly bak't will bring
The old Hag in. No surer thing.

Another Charme for Stables.[4]

HANG up Hooks, and Sheers to scare
    Hence the Hag, that rides the Mare,

---

[2] Folk-lore.   [3] Curious use of 'house'—to bring into your house. See last line.   [4] Folk-lore.

Till they be all over wet,
With the mire, and the sweat:
This observ'd, the Manes shall be
Of your horses, all knot-free.

Ceremonies for Candlemasse Eve.[5]

DOWN with the Rosemary and Bayes,
    Down with the Misleto;
Instead of Holly, now up-raise
    The greener Box[6] (for show.)

The Holly hitherto did sway;
    Let Box now domineere;
Untill the dancing Easter-day,
    Or Easters Eve appeare.

---

[5] In former times, foliage and flowers were much more frequently employed in the internal decoration of houses than at present; and different kinds were allotted to different seasons. The bay, holly, and misletoe, at Christmas, are not yet exploded. Strutt, in his *Manners and Customs of the English*, informs us, from Hollingshed, that our ancestors used to strew their houses with rushes, which were carefully spread over the floors, till carpets came in fashion; and it is still a practice to cover the ground with rushes in many churches, at Whitsuntide. N. The last custom has been finely celebrated by Wordsworth. See Notes and Queries, December 25th, 1875. The date is 1st February, or Eve of Purification of V. Mary.

[6] Boxwood plant.

Then youthfull Box which now hath grace,
    Your houses to renew;
Grown old, surrender must his place,
    Unto the crispèd Yew.

When Yew is out, then Birch comes in,
    And many Flowers beside;
Both of a fresh, and fragrant kinne
    To honour Whitsontide.

Green Rushes then, and sweetest Bents,[7]
    With cooler Oken boughs;
Come in for comely ornaments,
    To re-adorn the house.
Thus times do shift; each thing his turne do's hold;
New things succeed, as former things grow old.

The Ceremonies for Candlemasse day.[8]

KINDLE the Christmas Brand [9] and then
    Till Sunne-set, let it burne;
Which quencht, then lay it up agen,
    Till Christmas next returne.

---

[7] = long coarse moor growing grass.
[8] These two stanzas are curious, inasmuch as they record an old superstitious ceremony, which I do not recollect to have before met with. N.   [9] = Log.

Part must be kept wherewith to teend [1]
　　The Christmas Log next yeare;
And where 'tis safely kept, the Fiend,
　　Can do no mischiefe (there.)

Upon Candlemasse day.

END now the White-loafe, & the Pye,
　　And let all sports with Christmas dye.

Surfeits.

BAD are all surfeits : but Physitians call
That surfeit tooke by bread, the worst of all.

Upon Nis.

NIS, he makes Verses; but the Lines he writes,
Serve but for matter to make Paper-kites.

To Biancha, *to blesse him.*

WO'D I wooe, and wo'd I winne,
　　Wo'd I well my worke begin?
Wo'd I evermore be crown'd
With the end that I propound?
Wo'd I frustrate, or prevent
All Aspects malevolent?

---

[1] See Glossarial Index s. v.

Thwart all Wizzards, and with these
Dead all black contingencies :
Place my words, and all works else
In most happy Parallels?
All will prosper, if so be
I be kist, or blest by thee.

Julia's *Churching*, or *Purification*.

PUT on thy *Holy Fillitings*, and so
   To th' Temple with the sober *Midwife* go.
Attended thus (in a most solemn wise)
By those who serve the Child-bed misteries.
Burn first thine incense ; next, whenas thou see'st
The candid [2] Stole thrown ore the *Pious Priest;*
With reverend Curtsies come, and to him bring
Thy free (and not decurted [3]) offering.
All Rites well ended, with faire Auspice [4] come
(As to the breaking of a Bride-Cake) home :
Where ceremonious *Hymen* shall for thee
Provide a second *Epithalamie*.
She who keeps chastly to her husbands side
Is not for one, but every night his Bride :
And stealing still with love, and feare to Bed,
Brings him not one, but many a Maiden-head.

---

   [2] = white.   [3] = shortened : used now only in 'curt' and 'curtly.'
   [4] See Glossarial Index s. v.

To his Book.

BEFORE the Press scarce one co'd see
    A little-peeping-part of thee:
But since th' art Printed, thou dost call
To shew thy nakedness to all.
My care for thee is now the less,
(Having resign'd thy shamefac'tness:)
Go with thy Faults and Fates; yet stay
And take this sentence, then away;
Whom one belov'd will not suffice,
She'l runne to all adulteries.

Teares.

TEARES most prevaile; with teares too thou
    mayst move
Rocks to relent, and coyest maids to love.

To his friend to avoid contention of words.

WORDS beget Anger; Anger brings forth blowes:
    Blowes make of dearest friends immortall Foes.
For which prevention (Sociate [5]) let there be
Betwixt us two no more *Logomachie*.[6]
Farre better 'twere for either to be mute,
Then for to murder friendship, by dispute.   *[than*

---

[5] = companion, friend.   [6] = war of words.

Truth.

TRUTH is best found out by the time, and eyes;
   Falsehood winnes credit by uncertainties.

Upon Prickles. *Epig.*

PRICKLES is waspish, and puts forth his sting,
  For Bread, Drinke, Butter, Cheese; for every
    thing
That *Prickles* buyes, puts *Prickles* out of frame;
How well his nature's fitted to his name!

The Eyes before the Eares.

WE credit most our sight; one eye doth please
  Our trust farre more then ten eare-witnesses.
                              [*than*

Want.

WANT is a softer Wax, that takes thereon,
  This, that, and every base impression.

To a Friend.

LOOKE in my Book, and herein see,
  Life endlesse sign'd to thee and me.
We o're the tombes, and Fates shall flye;
While other generations dye.

Upon M. William Lawes, *the rare Musitian.*[7]

SHO'D I not put on Blacks, when each one here
  Comes with his Cypresse, and devotes a teare?
Sho'd I not grieve (my *Lawes*) when every Lute,
Violl, and Voice, is (by thy losse) struck mute?
Thy loss, brave man! whose Numbers have been
    hurl'd,
And no less prais'd, then spread throughout the
    world.   [*tha1*
Some have Thee call'd *Amphion;* some of us,
Nam'd thee *Terpander*, or sweet *Orpheus:*
Some this, some that, but all in this agree,
Musique had both her birth and death with Thee.

A Song upon Silvia.

FROM me my *Silvia* ranne away,
    And running therewithall,
A *Primrose* Banke did cross her way,
    And gave my Love a fall.

But trust me now, I dare not say,
    What I by chance did see;
But such the Drap'ry did betray
    That fully ravisht me.

[7] See Memorial-Introduction.

The Hony-combe.

IF thou hast found an honie-combe,
  Eate thou not all, but taste on some:
For if thou eat'st it to excess;
That sweetness turnes to Loathsomness.
Taste it to Temper [8]; then 'twill be
Marrow, and Manna unto thee.

Vpon Ben. Johnson. [9]

HERE lyes *Johnson* with the rest
  Of the Poets; but the Best.
Reader, wo'dst thou more have known?
Aske his Story, not this Stone.
That will speake what this can't tell
Of his glory. *So farewell.*

An Ode for him.

AH *Ben!*
  Say how, or when
Shall we thy Guests
Meet at those *Lyrick* Feasts,
  Made at the *Sun,*
The *Dog,* the triple *Tunne?*

---

[8] = temperance, moderation.   [9] On this and next see Memorial-Introduction.

Where we such clusters had,
As made us nobly wild, not mad;
And yet each Verse of thine
Out-did the meate, out-did the frolick wine.

My *Ben !*
Or come agen :
Or send to us,
Thy wits great over-plus ;
But teach us yet
Wisely to husband it ;
Lest we that Tallent spend :
And having once brought to an end
That precious stock ; the store
Of such a wit the world sho'd have no more.

Upon a Virgin.

SPEND Harmless shade, thy nightly Houres,
Selecting here, both Herbs, and Flowers ;
Of which make Garlands here, and there,
To dress thy silent sepulchre.
Nor do thou feare the want of these,
In everlasting Properties.
Since we fresh strewings will bring hither,
Farre faster then the first can wither. [*than*

Blame.

IN Battailes what disasters fall,
　　The King he beares the blame of all.

A request to the Graces.

PONDER my words, if so that any be
　　Known guilty here of incivility:
Let what is graceless, discompos'd, and rude,
With sweetness, smoothness, softness, be endu'd.
Teach it to blush, to curtsie, lisp, and shew
Demure, but yet, full of temptation too.
Numbers ne'r tickle, or but lightly please,
Unlesse they have some wanton carriages.[1]
This if ye do, each Piece will here be good,
And gracefull made, by your neate[2] Sisterhood.

Upon himselfe.

I LATELY fri'd,[3] but now behold
　　I freeze as fast, and shake for cold.

---

[1] Thus the poet of Verona, in a similar strain:—
　　　　Nam castum esse decet pium poetam
　　　　Ipsum: versiculos nihil necesse est:
　　　　Qui tum denique habent salem ac leporem,
　　　　Si sunt molliculi, ac parum pudici,
　　　　Et quod pruriat, incitare possunt.
　　　　　　　　　　　　Catul. Carmen 16. N.
[2] = elegant.　　[3] See Glossarial Index under 'frie.'

And in good faith I'd thought it strange
T'ave found in me this sudden change;
But that I understood by dreames,
These only were but Loves extreames;
Who fires with hope the Lovers heart,
And starves with cold the self-same part.

Multitude.

WE Trust not to the multitude in Warre,
   But to the stout; and those that skilfull are.

Feare.

MAN must do well out of a good intent;
   Not for the servile feare[4] of punishment.

To M. Kellam.[5]

WHAT! can my *Kellam* drink his Sack
   In Goblets to the brim,
And see his *Robin Herrick* lack,
   Yet send no Boules to him?

---

[4] "Oderunt peccare boni virtutis amore:
   Tu nihil admittes in te fomidine pœnae."
              Horace: Epist. i. xvi. 10, ll 52-3.

[5] A parishioner, probably.

For love or pitie to his Muse,
    (That she may flow in Verse)
Contemne to recommend a Cruse,
    But send to her a Tearce.[6]

Happinesse to hospitalitie, or a hearty to good house-keeping.

FIRST, may the hand of bounty bring
    Into the daily offering
Of full provision; such a store,
Till that the Cooke cries, Bring no more.
Upon your hogsheads never fall
A drought of wine, ale, beere (at all;)
But, like full clouds, may they from thence
Diffuse their mighty influence.
Next, let the Lord, and Ladie here
Enjoy a Christning yeare by yeare;
And this *good blessing* back them still,
T'ave Boyes, and Gyrles too, as they will.
Then from the porch may many a Bride
Unto the Holy Temple ride:
And thence return, (short prayers seyd)
A wife most richly marri èd.

---

[6] = cask, one-third of a pipe, 42 gallons.

Last, may the Bride and Bridegroome be
Untoucht by cold *sterility* ;
But in their springing blood so play,
As that in *Lusters* few they may,
By laughing too, and lying downe,
People a *City* or a *Towne*.

Cunctation[7] *in Correction.*

THE *Lictors*[8] bundl'd up their rods : beside,
  Knit them with knots (with much adoe unty'd)
That if (unknitting) men wo'd yet repent,
They might escape the lash of punishment.

Present Government grievous.

MEN *are suspicious ; prone to discontent :*
  Subjects still loath the present Government.[9]

Rest Refreshes.

LAY by the good a while ; a resting field
  Will, after ease, a richer harvest yeild :
Trees this year beare ; next, they their wealth with-
        hold :
Continuall reaping makes a land wax old.

---

[7] =delay.   [8] =ligatores?
[9] So Hooker begins his "Ecclesiastical Polity.'

Revenge.

MANS disposition is for to requite
 An injurie, before a benefite:
Thanksgiving is a burden,[1] and a paine;
Revenge is pleasing to us, as our gaine.

The first marrs or makes.

IN all our high designments, 'twill appeare,
 The first event breeds confidence or feare.

Beginning, difficult.

HARD are the two first staires unto a Crowne;
 Which got, the third, bids him a King come downe.

Faith four-square.[2]

FAITH is a thing that's four-square; let it fall
 This way or that, it not declines at all.

---

[1] Cf. the remarks by which Reynolds attracted the notice of Dr. Johnson: "You have the comfort of being released from a burden of gratitude." (Boswell sub. anno, 1752.)

[2] See Glossarial Index s. v.

The present time best pleaseth.

PRAISE they that will Times past, I joy to see
My selfe now live : *this age best pleaseth mee.*

Cloathes, are conspirators.

THOUGH from without no foes at all we feare ;
We shall be wounded by the cloathes we weare.

Cruelty.

TIS *but a dog-like madnesse in bad Kings,*
    For to delight in wounds and murderings.
As some plants prosper best by cuts and blowes ;
So Kings by killing doe encrease their foes.

Faire after foule.

TEARES *quickly drie : griefes will in time decay :*
    A cleare, will come after a cloudy, day.

Hunger.

ASKE me what hunger is, and Ile reply,
    'Tis but a fierce desire of hot and drie.

Bad wages for good service.

IN this misfortune Kings doe most excell,
    To heare the worst from men, when they doe well.

The End.

CONQUER we shall, but we must first contend;
 '*Tis not the Fight that crowns us, but the end.*[3]

The Bondman.

BIND me but to thee with thine haire,
    And quickly I shall be
Made by that fetter or that snare
    A bondman unto thee.

Or if thou tak'st that bond away,
    Then bore me through the eare;
And by the Law [4] I ought to stay
    For ever with thee here.

Choose for the best.

GIVE house-roome to the best; '*Tis never known
Vertue and pleasure, both to dwell in one.*

To Silvia.

PARDON my trespasse (Silvia,) I confesse,
    My kisse out-went the bounds of shamfastnesse:
None is discreet at all times; no, *not Jove
Himselfe, at one time, can be wise and Love.*

---

[3] "*Finis coronat opus*" (a Proverb).   [4] See Exodus xxi. 6.

Faire shewes deceive.

SMOOTH was the Sea, and seem'd to call
   To prettie girles to play withall:
Who padling there, the Sea soone frown'd,
And on a sudden both were drown'd.
What credit can we give to seas,
Who, kissing, kill such Saints as these?

His wish.

FAT be my Hinde; unlearnèd be my wife;
   Peacefull my night; my day devoid of strife:
To these a comely off-spring I desire,
Singing about my everlasting fire.

Upon Julia's *washing her self in the river.*

HOW fierce was I, when I did see
   My *Julia* wash her self in thee!
So *Lillies* thorough Christall look:
So purest pebbles in the brook:
As in the River *Julia* did,
Halfe with a Lawne of water hid,
Into thy streames my self I threw,
And strugling there, I kist thee too;
And more had done (it is confest)
Had not thy waves forbad the rest.

A Meane in our Meanes.

THOUGH Frankinsense the *Deities* require,
  We must not give all to the hallowed fire.
Such be our gifts, and such be our expence,
As for our selves to leave some frankinsence.[5]

Upon Clunn.

A ROWLE of Parchment *Clunn* about him beares,
  Charg'd with the Armes of all his Ancestors:
And seems halfe ravisht, when he looks upon
That Bar, this *Bend*; that *Fess*, this *Cheveron*;
This *Manch*, that *Moone*; this *Martlet*, and that
  Mound;
This counterchange of *Perle* and *Diamond*.[6]
What joy can *Clun* have in that Coat, or this,
Whenas his owne still out at elboes is?

Upon Cupid.[7]

LOVE, like a Beggar, came to me
  With Hose and Doublet torne:

---

[5] " Sure none need be more bountifull in giving then the Sunne is in shining, which though freely bestowing his beames on the world keeps notwithstanding the body of light to himself. Yea it is necessary that Liberality should as well have banks as a stream."
        Fuller's Holy and Profane State (1648), p. 29.

[6] = mode of blazon sometimes used in case of Peers. The others are also heraldic terms.

[7] Our poet has before pourtrayed a fairy beggar. He now gives us

His Shirt bedangling from his knee,
    With Hat and Shooes out-worne.

He askt an almes; I gave him bread,
    And meat too, for his need:
Of which, when he had fully fed,
    He wished me all *Good speed*.

Away he went, but as he turn'd
    (In faith I know not how)
He toucht me so, as that I burn,
    And am tormented now.

Love's silent flames, and fires obscure
    Then crept into my heart;
And though I saw no Bow, I'm sure,
    His finger was the dart.

Vpon Blisse.

BLISSE (last night drunk) did kisse his mothers
    knee:
Where he will kisse (next drunk) conjecture ye.

Vpon Burr.

BURR is a smell-feast, and a man alone,
    That (where meat is) will be a hanger on.

Love in a mendicant form. The style of this little Anacreontic sketch will somewhat remind us of the third Ode of the sportive Teian. N.

Vpon Megg.

MEGG yesterday was troubled with a Pose,
  Which, this night hardned, sodders up her nose.[8]

An Hymne to Love.

1.
    I WILL confesse
    With Cheerfulnesse,
Love is a thing so likes me,
    That let her lay
    On me all day,
Ile kiss the hand that strikes me.

2.
    I will not, I
    Now blubb'ring, cry,
It (Ah!) too late repents me,
    That I did fall
    To love at all,
Since love so much contents me.

3.
    No, no, Ile be
    In fetters free :
While others they sit wringing
    Their hands for paine ;
    Ile entertaine
The wounds of love with singing.

[8] = rheum—a cold in the head.

4. With Flowers and Wine,
    And Cakes Divine,
To strike me I will tempt thee:
    Which done; no more
    Ile come before
Thee and thine Altars emptie.

To his honoured and most ingenious friend
Mr. Charles Cotton.[9]

FOR brave comportment, wit without offence,
    Words fully flowing, yet of influence:
Thou art that man of men, the man alone,
Worthy the Publique Admiration:
Who with thine owne eyes read'st what we doe write,
And giv'st our Numbers *Euphonie*, and weight.
Tel'st when a Verse springs high, how understood
To be, or not borne of the Royall-blood.
What State above, what *Symmetrie* below,
Lines have, or sho'd have, thou the best canst show.
For which (my *Charles*) it is my pride to be,
Not so much knowne, as to be lov'd of thee.
Long may I live so, and my wreath of *Bayes*,
Be lesse anothers *Laurell*, then thy praise.   [*than*

[9] The translator of Montaigne and associate of Isaak Walton.

HESPERIDES.

Women uselesse.

WHAT need we marry Women, when
    Without their use we may have men?
And such as will in short time be,
For murder fit, or mutinie;
As *Cadmus* once a new way found,
By throwing teeth into the ground;[10]
(From which poore seed, and rudely sown)
Sprung up a War-like Nation.
So let us Yron, Silver, Gold,
Brasse, Leade, or Tinne, throw into th' mould;
And we shall see in little space
Rise up of men, a fighting race.
If this can be, say then, what need
Have we of Women or their seed?

Love is a sirrup.

LOVE is a sirrup; and who er'e we see
    Sick and surcharg'd with this sacietie:[1]
Shall by this pleasing trespasse quickly prove,
Ther's loathsomnesse[2] e'en in the sweets of love.

[10] Ovid, Metamorph.   [1] = satiety.
[2] "Medio de fonte leporum
    surgit amari aliquid." Lucretius.

Leven.[3]

LOVE is a Leven, and a loving kisse
   The Leven of a loving sweet-heart is.

Repletion.

PHYSITIANS say Repletion springs
   More from the sweet then sower things. [than

On Himselfe.

WEEPE for the dead, for they have lost this
   light :
And weepe for me, lost in an endlesse night.
Or mourne, or make a Marble Verse for me,
Who writ for many. *Benedicite.*

No Man without Money.

NO man such rare parts hath, that he can swim,
   If favour or occasion helpe not him.

On Himselfe.

LOST to the world ; lost to my selfe ; alone
   Here now I rest under this Marble stone :
In depth of silence, heard, and seene of none.

---

[3] = leaven.

To M. Leonard Willan [4] *his*
peculiar friend.

I WILL be short, and having quickly hurl'd
  This line about, live Thou throughout the world;
Who art a man for all Sceanes;[5] unto whom
(What's hard to others) nothing's troublesome.
Can'st write the *Comick, Tragick* straine, and fall
From these to penne the pleasing Pastorall:
Who fli'st at all heights: Prose and Verse run'st
  through;
Find'st here a fault, and mend'st the trespasse too:
For which I might extoll thee, but speake lesse,
Because thy selfe art comming to the Presse:
And then sho'd I in praising thee be slow,
Posterity will pay thee what I owe.

To his worthy Friend M. John Hall,
  Student of Grayes-Inne.[6]

TELL me, young man, or did the Muses bring
  Thee lesse to taste, then to drink up their
    Spring;
That none hereafter sho'd be thought, or be
A Poet, or a Poet-like but Thee?

---

[4] Nothing seems to be known of this Willan in dramatic history.
[5] See Glossarial Index s. v.   [6] See Memorial-Introduction.

What was thy Birth, thy starre that makes thee
    knowne,
At twice ten yeares, a prime and publike one?
Tell us thy Nation, kindred, or the whence
Thou had'st, and hast thy *mighty influence,*
That makes thee lov'd, and of the men desir'd,
And no lesse prais'd, then of the maides admir'd. [*than*
Put on thy Laurell then; and in that trimme
Be thou *Apollo*, or the type of him:
Or let the *Unshorne God* lend thee his Lyre,
And next to him, be Master of the Quire.

To Julia.

OFFER thy gift; but first the Law commands
    Thee, *Julia*, first, to *sanctifie* thy hands:
Doe that, my *Julia* which the rites require,
Then boldly give thine incense to the fire.

To the most comely and proper
M. Elizabeth Finch.[7]

HANSOME you are, and Proper you will be
    Despight of all your infortunitie:[8]

---

[7] Sir Moyle Finch, 1st Baronet of Eastwell, co. Kent, had a d. Elizabeth, who died young, but there were others of the name, so that it would be unsafe to identify this M. Elizabeth Finch.

[8] = ill fortune.

Live long and lovely, but yet grow no lesse
In that your owne prefixèd comelinesse:
Spend on that stock: and when your life must fall,
Leave others Beauty, to set up withall.

Upon Ralph.

RALPH pares his nayles, his warts, his cornes, and *Ralph*
In sev'rall tills and boxes, keepes 'em safe;
Instead of Harts-horne (if he speakes the troth)
To make a lustie-gellie [9] for his broth.

To his Booke.

IF hap it must, that I must see thee lye
 Absyrtus-like,[1] all torne confusedly:
With solemne tears, and with much grief of heart,
Ile recollect thee (weeping) part by part;
And having washt thee, close thee in a chest
With spice; that done, Ile leave thee to thy rest.

---

[9] = jelly, condiment.
[1] Absyrtus, son of the king of Colchis, torn to pieces by Medea when she fled with Jason.

TO THE KING,

Upon his welcome to Hampton-Court.
Set and Sung.[2]

WELCOME, *Great Cesar*, welcome now you are,
  As dearest Peace, after destructive Warre:
Welcome as slumbers; or as beds of ease
After our long, and peevish sicknesses.
O *Pompe of Glory!* Welcome now, and come
To re-possess once more your long'd-for home.
A thousand Altars smoake; a thousand thighes
Of Beeves here ready stand for Sacrifice.
Enter and prosper; while our eyes doe waite
For an *Ascendent* throughly *Auspicate*:[3]
Under which signe we may the former stone
Lay of our safeties new foundation:
That done; *O Cesar!* live, and be to us,
Our *Fate*, our *Fortune*, and our *Genius*;
To whose free knees we may our temples tye
As to a still protecting Deitie:

---

[2] The King was settled at Hampton Court under the protection of the army, Aug. 24, 1647: but this poem seems to celebrate an earlier and happier occasion.

[3] Term of Astrology: a rising of such part of the ecliptic as may be auspicious.

That sho'd you stirre, we and our Altars too
May *(Great Augustus) goe along with You.*
Chor. Long live the King; and to accomplish this,
We'l from our owne, adde far more years to his.

Ultimus Heroum :
or, *To the most Learned, and to the right Honourable,*
Henry, *Marquesse of* Dorchester.[4]

AND as time past when *Cato* the Severe
    Entred the circum-spacious Theater;
In reverence of his person, every one
Stood as he had been turn'd from flesh to stone:
E'ne so my numbers will astonisht be
If but lookt on; struck dead, if scan'd by Thee.

To his Muse, another to the same.

TELL that Brave Man, fain thou wo'dst have access
To kiss his hands, but that for fearfullness;
Or else because th' art like a modest Bride,
Ready to blush to death, sho'd he but chide.

---

[4] Henry Pierrepont, 2nd Earl of Kingston, was created Marquis of Dorchester, 25th March, 1644. He died in 1680. He was eldest son of the " brave Newark."

Upon Vineger.

VINEGER is no other I define,
  Then the dead Corps, or Carkase of the Wine. [*than*

Upon Mudge.[5]

MUDGE every morning to the Postern comes,
  (His teeth all out) to rince and wash his gummes.

To his learned Friend M. Jo. Harmar,[6]
Phisitian to the Colledge of Westminster.

WHEN first I find those Numbers thou do'st write,
To be most soft, terce, sweet, and perpolite :[7]
Next, when I see Thee towring in the skie,
In an expansion no less large, then high ; [*than*
Then, in that compass, sayling here and there,
And with Circumgyration[8] every where ;

---

[5] A Devonshire name.

[6] A native of Churchdoune, co. Gloucester: M. A. at Oxford in 1617, and (according to Anthony a-Wood) was always afterwards called "Doctor," though he had taken no higher degree than M. A). He was sometime under-master of Westminster School, and Herrick no doubt playfully transmuted "Doctor" into "physician." He wrote Latin verse: died 1st Nov., 1670.   [7] = thoroughly polished.

[8] See Glossarial Index under 'circum.'

Following with love and active heate thy game,
And then at last to truss [9] the Epigram ;
I must confess, distinction none I see
Between *Domitians Martiall*[1] then, and Thee.
But this I know, should *Jupiter* agen
Descend from heaven, to re-converse with men :
The Romane Language full, and superfine,
If *Jove* wo'd speake, he wo'd accept of thine.

Upon his Spaniell Tracie.[2]

NOW thou art dead, no eye shall ever see,
   For shape and service, *Spaniell* like to thee.
This shall my love doe, give thy sad death one
Teare, that deserves of me a million.

The Deluge.

DROWNING, drowning, I espie
   Coming from my *Julia's* eye :
'Tis some solace in our smart,
To have friends to beare a part :
I have none ; but must be sure
Th' inundation to endure.

---

[9] As the whole metaphor is a hawking one, 'truss' must here mean, to seize and carry aloft.   [1] Domitiani Martiall.
[2] See Glossarial Index.

Shall not times hereafter tell
This for no meane *miracle;*
When the waters by their fall
Threatn'd ruine unto all?
Yet the deluge here was known,
Of a world to drowne but One.

Upon Lupes.

LUPES for the outside of his suite has paide;
   But for his heart, he cannot have it made:
The reason is, his credit cannot get
The inward carbage [3] for his cloathes as yet.

Raggs.

WHAT are our patches, tatters, raggs, and rents,
   But the base dregs and lees of vestiments?

Strength to support Soveraignty.

LET Kings and Rulers learne this line from me;
   Where power is weake, unsafe is Majestie.

Upon Tubbs.

FOR thirty yeares, *Tubbs* has been proud and poor;
'Tis now his habit, which he can't give ore.

   [3] = garbage, as from 'garb,' trimming.

Crutches.

THOU seest me *Lucia* this year droope,
    Three *Zodiaks* fill'd more I shall stoope;
Let Crutches then provided be
To shore[4] up my debilitie.
Then while thou laugh'st; Ile, sighing, crie,
A *Ruine underpropt* am I:
Do'n[5] will I then my *Beadsmans*[6] gown,
And when so feeble I am grown,
As my weake shoulders cannot beare
The burden of a *Grashopper*:
Yet with the bench of aged sires,
When I and they keep tearmly fires;[7]
With my weake voice I'le sing, or say
Some Odes I made of *Lucia*:[8]

---

[4] = support.   [5] Note the transition-form ' D'on ' = do on.

[6] An almsman, or one that prays for a benefactor. Selden says, in his *Titles of Honour*, that he had seen a petition from a bishop to our king, Henry V., subscribed with " your worship's beadsman." Glossographia. N. Burns signed himself in a charming poem, " The beadsman of Nithsdale."

[7] This couplet may imply a wish to spend his old age with his former ancestors at the college where he was educated, or afterwards resided.

[8] From the preceding mention of the grasshopper, connected with his weak voice, it may be presumed that our poet had in view Homer's similitude with respect to feeble garrulous old men, in his third Iliad: ἀλλ' ἀγορηταὶ, &c. N. The reference is rather to Ecclesiastes xii. 5.

Then will I heave my wither'd hand
To *Jove* the Mighty, for to stand
Thy faithfull friend, and to poure downe
Upon thee many a *Benizon*.

To Julia.

HOLY waters hither bring
   For the sacred sprinkling:
Baptize me and thee, and so
Let us to the Altar go.
And (ere we our rites commence)
Wash our hands in innocence.
Then I'le be the *Rex Sacrorum*,
Thou the Queen of *Peace and Quorum.*[9]

Upon Case.

CASE is a Lawyer, that near pleads alone,   [*nere*
   But when he hears the like confusion,
As when the disagreeing Commons throw
About their House, their clamorous I,[1] or No:
Then *Case*, as loud as any *Serjant* there,
Cries out (My lord, my Lord) the Case is clear:
But when all's hush't, *Case* then a fish more mute,[2] [*than*
Bestirs his Hand, but starves in hand the Suite.

[9] =of Peace and *Law*.   [1] See Glossarial Index s. v.
[2] A classical epithet ἔλλος.

To Perenna.

I A *Dirge* will pen for thee ;
  Thou a *Trentall*³ make for me :
That the Monks and Fryers together,
Here may sing the rest of either :
Next, I'm sure, the Nuns will have
Candlemas to grace the Grave.

To his Sister in Law, *M*. Susanna Herrick.⁴

THE Person crowns the Place ; your lot doth fall
  Last, yet to be with These a Principall.
Howere it fortuned ; know for Truth, I meant
You a fore-leader in this Testament.

Upon the Lady Crew.⁵

THIS Stone can tell the storie of my life,
  What was my Birth, to whom I was a Wife :
In teeming years, how soon my Sun was set,
Where now I rest, these may be known by *Jet*.⁶
For other things, my many Children be
The best and truest *Chronicles* of me.

---

³ See Glossarial Index s. v.   ⁴ See Memorial-Introduction.
⁵ She died 2nd December, 1639.   See the various Crewe poems.
⁶ Qu—ink ? or the black-painted inscription ? or the jet-black marble or other stone ?

On Tomasin Parsons.[7]
GROW up in Beauty, as thou do'st begin,
 And be of all admirèd, *Tomasin*.

Ceremony upon Candlemas Eve.
DOWN with the Rosemary, and so
 Down with the Baies, & misletoe:
Down with the Holly, Ivie, all,
Wherewith ye drest the Christmas Hall:
That so the superstitious find
No one least Branch there left behind:
For look, how many leaves there be
Neglected there (maids trust to me)
So many *Goblins* you shall see.[8]

Suspicion makes secure.
HE that will live of all cares dispossest,
 Must shun the bad, I,[9] and suspect the best.

Upon Spokes.
SPOKES, when he sees a rosted Pig, he swears
 Nothing he loves on't but the chaps and ears:
But carve to him the fat flanks; and he shall
Rid these, and those, and part by part eat all.

---

[7] A forgotten woman ('Thomasina').   [8] Folk-lore.
[9] =ay, as before.

To his Kinsman, M. Tho : Herrick, *who desired to be in his Book.*[10]

WELCOME to this my Colledge, and though late
   Th'ast got a place here (standing candidate)
It matters not, since thou art chosen one
Here of my great and good foundation.

A Bucolick betwixt Two : Lacon *and* Thyrsis.[1]

Lacon. FOR a kiss or two, confesse,
      What doth cause this pensiveness,
   Thou most lovely Neat-heardesse ?[2]
   Why so lonely on the hill ?
   Why thy pipe by thee so still,
   That erewhile was heard so shrill ?
   Tell me, do thy kine now fail
   To fulfill [3] the milkin-paile ?
   Say, what is't that thou do'st aile ?

Thyr. None of these ; but out, alas !
   A mischance is come to pass,
   And I'le tell thee what it was :
   See mine eyes are weeping ripe,

---

[10] See Memorial-Introduction.

[1] Thyrsis in this poem is applied to a female character. I do not recollect to have seen it before given to a shepherdess by any pastoral writer. [2] = Cattle shepherdess. [3] See Glossarial Index s. v.

Lacon. Tell, and I'le lay down my Pipe.

Thyr. I have lost my lovely steere,
That to me was far more deer
Then these kine, which I milke here. [*than*
Broad of fore-head, large of eye,
Party-colour'd like a Pie; [4]
Smooth in each limb as a die;
Clear of hoof, and clear of horn;
Sharply pointed as a thorn:
With a neck by yoke unworn.
From the which hung down by strings,
Balls of Cowslips, Daisie rings,
Enterplac't with ribbanings.
Faultless every way for shape;
Not a straw co'd him escape;
Ever gamesome as an ape:
But yet harmless as a sheep.
(Pardon, *Lacon* if I weep)
Tears will spring, where woes are deep.
Now (ai me!) (ai me!) Last night
Came a mad dog, and did bite,
I,[5] and kil'd my dear delight.

Lacon. Alack, for grief!

[4] = pye.   [5] = ay.

Thyr. But I'le be brief.
Hence I must, for time doth call
Me, and my sad Play-mates all,
To his Ev'ning Funerall.
Live long, *Lacon,* so *adew!*

Lacon. Mournfull maid, farewell to you;
Earth afford ye flowers to strew.

Upon Sapho.

LOOK upon *Sapho's* lip, and you will swear,
There is a love-like leven [6] rising there.

Upon Faunus.

WE read how *Faunus,*[7] he the shepheards *God,*
His wife to death whipt with a *Mirtle Rod.*
The Rod (perhaps) was better'd by the name;
But had it been of Birch, the death's the same.

The Quintell.[8]

UP with the Quintill, that the Rout,
May fart for joy, as well as shout:
Either's welcome, Stinke or Civit,
If we take it, as they give it.

[6] Leaven.   [7] Mythical.
[8] See Glossarial Index. There used to be a Quintain Club at Oxford (1830-49), chiefly supported by the wealthier under-graduate members of Christ's Church.

A Bachanalian Verse.

1. DRINKE up
    Your Cup,
 But not spill Wine ;
    For if you
        Do,
 'Tis an ill signe ;

2.   That we
        Foresee,
 You are cloy'd here,
    If so, no
        Hoe,[9]
 But avoid here.

Care a good keeper.

CARE keepes the Conquest ; *'tis no lesse renowne,*
 To keepe a Citie, then to winne a Towne.

Rules for our reach.

MEN must have Bounds[10] how farre to walke; for we
 Are made farre worse, by lawless liberty.

---

[9] Cf. 'Ho' in Halliwell : =stop.
[10] " Est modus in rebus," &c., Horace, Sat. i. 1, 106-7: Ep. i, 1, 32.

To Biancha.

AH *Biancha!* now I see,
    It is Noone and past with me:
In a while it will strike one;
Then, *Biancha,* I am gone.
Some *effusions* [1] let me have,
Offer'd on my holy Grave;
Then, *Biancha,* let me rest
With my face towards the East.[2]

To the handsome Mistresse Grace Potter.[3]

AS is your name, so is your comely face,
    Toucht everywhere with such diffusèd grace,
As that in all that *admirable round,*
There is not one least *solecisme* found;
And as that part, so every portion else,
Keepes line for line with *Beauties Parallels.*

Anacreontike.

I MUST
    Not trust
Here to any;
    Bereav'd,
    Deceiv'd

---

[1] = outpourings.

[2] The usual position—to salute the Sun of Righteousness at the Resurrection.   [3] See Memorial-Introduction.

By so many :
   As one
   Undone
By my losses ;
   Comply
   Will I
With my crosses.
   Yet still
   I will
Not be grieving ;
   Since thence
   And hence
Comes relieving.
   But this
   Sweet is
In our mourning ;
   Times bad
   And sad
Are a turning :
   And he
   Whom we
See dejected ;
   Next day
   Wee may
See erected.

More modest, more manly.

'TIS still observ'd, those men most valiant are,
  That are most modest ere they come to warre.

Not to covet much where little is the charge.

WHY sho'd we covet much, whenas we know,
  W'ave more to beare our charge, then way
    to go?   [*than*

Anacreontick Verse.

BRISK methinks I am, and fine,
  When I drinke my capring [4] wine:
Then to love I do encline,
When I drinke my wanton wine:
And I wish all maidens mine,
When I drinke my sprightly wine:
Well I sup, and well I dine,
When I drinke my frolick wine:
But I languish, lowre, and Pine,
When I want my fragrant wine.

Upon Pennie.

BROWN bread *Tom Pennie* eates, and must of right,
  Because his stock will not hold out for white.

---

[4] = leaping, sparkling, with the under-thought, that inclines him to dance or 'caper' and be merry. So when he drinks of the wanton making wine he inclines to love, &c., &c.

Patience in Princes.

KINGS must not use the Axe for each offence:
Princes cure some faults by their patience.

Feare gets force.

DESPAIRE takes heart, when ther's no hope to
    speed:
The Coward then takes Armes, and do's the deed.

Parcell-gil't-Poetry.

LET'S strive to be the best; the Gods, we know it,
    Pillars and men, hate an indifferent Poet.

Upon Love, by way of question and answer.

I BRING ye Love.   *Quest.* What will love do?
    Ans. Like, and dislike ye:
I bring ye love: *Quest.* What will Love do?
    Ans. Stroake ye to strike ye.
I bring ye love: *Quest.* What will Love do?
    Ans. Love will be-foole ye:
I bring ye love: *Quest.* What will love do?
    Ans. Heate ye to coole ye:
I bring ye love: *Quest.* What will love do?
    Ans. Love gifts will send ye:

I bring ye love :   *Quest.* What will love do ?
    Ans. Stock ye to spend ye :
I bring ye love :   *Quest.* What will love do ?
    Ans. Love will fulfill ye :
I bring ye love :   *Quest.* What will love do ?
    Ans. Kisse ye, to kill ye.

To the Lord Hopton, *on his fight in* Cornwall.[5]

GO on, brave *Hopton*, to effectuate that
    Which wee, and times to come, shall wonder at.
Lift up thy Sword ; next, suffer it to fall,
And by that *One blow* set an end to all.

His Grange.

HOW well contented in this private *Grange*
    Spend I my life (that's subject unto change :)
Under whose Roofe with *Mosse-worke* wrought,
    there I
Kisse my *Brown wife,* and *black Posterity.*

---

[5] Sir Ralph Hopton, of Stratton, co. Cornwall : created a Knight of the Bath at the coronation of Charles I. He took up arms in the Royal cause in 1642, and distinguished himself in several military affairs, but especially at Bradock Down, Stratton, where he obtained a decisive victory, and was in consequence created Baron Hopton 4th Sep., 1643. He went abroad during the Commonwealth, and died at Bruges in 1652. Of course Herrick inserted the later title on publishing his book.

Leprosie in houses.

WHEN to a House I come, and see
    The *Genius* wastefull, more then free :   [*than*
The servants *thumblesse*,[6] yet to eat,
With lawlesse tooth the floure of wheate :
The Sonnes to suck the milke of Kine,
More then the teats of Discipline :
The Daughters wild and loose in dresse ;
Their cheekes unstain'd with shamefac'tnesse :
The Husband drunke, the Wife to be
A Baud to incivility :[7]
I must confesse, I there descrie,
A House spred through with *Leprosie*.

Good Manners at meat.

THIS rule of manners I will teach my guests,
    To come with their own bellies unto feasts :
Not to eat equall portions ; but to rise
Farc't[8] with the food, that may themselves suffice.

---

[6] Qu—awkward, unhandy ? or from his former use of '*painful* thumb' it may be negligent, idle. See Glossarial Index s. v.

[7] = a harbourer and promoter of incivility or unmannerliness.

[8] = stuffed.

Anthea's *Retractation*.

ANTHEA laught, and fearing lest excesse
    Might stretch the cords of civill comelinesse:
She with a dainty blush rebuk't her face;
And cal'd each line back to his *rule* and *space*.

Comforts in Crosses.

BE not dismaide, though crosses cast thee downe;
    Thy fall is but the rising to a Crowne.

Seeke and finde.[9]

ATTEMPT the end, and never stand to doubt;
    Nothing's so hard, but search will find it out.

Rest.

ON with thy worke, though thou beest hardly
    prest;
Labour is held up, by the hope of rest.[1]

---

[9] Improbus. "Labor omnia vincit." Georgic i.
[1] ——— "hac mente laborem
    Sese ferri, senes ut in otia tuta recedant,
    Aiunt."   Horace, Sat. i. 1, 30-2.

Leprosie in Cloathes.

WHEN flowing garments I behold
    Enspir'd[2] with *Purple, Pearle,* and *Gold;*
I think no other but I see
In them a glorious leprosie,
That do's infect, and make the rent
More mortall in the vestiment.
As flowrie vestures doe descrie[3]
The wearers rich immodestie;
So plaine and simple cloathes doe show
Where vertue walkes, not those that flow.

Upon Buggins.

B*UGGINS* is Drunke all night, all day he sleepe
    This is the Levell-coyle[4] that *Buggins* keeps.

Great Maladies, long Medicines.

T*O an old soare a long cure must goe on ;*
    Great faults require great satisfaction.

His Answer to a friend.

YOU aske me what I doe, and how I live?
    And (Noble friend) this answer I must give:

---

[2] = encircled with borderings of purple, &c. (σπειρα spira).
[3] = discover or reveal.   [4] See Glossarial Index s. v.

Drooping, I draw on to the vaults of death,
Or'e which you'l walk, when I am laid beneath.

The Begger.

SHALL I a daily Begger be,
   For loves sake asking almes of thee?
Still shall I crave, and never get
A hope of my desirèd bit?
Ah cruell maides! Ile goe my way,
Whereas (perchance) my fortunes may
Finde out a Threshold or a doore,
That may far sooner speed the poore:
Where thrice we knock, and none will heare,
Cold comfort still I'm sure lives there.

Bastards.

OUR Bastard-children are but like to Plate,
   Made by the Coyners illegitimate.

His change.

MY many cares and much distress,
   Has made me like a wilderness:
Or (discompos'd) I'm like a rude,
And all-confusèd multitude:
Out of my comely manners worne;
And as in meanes, in minde all torne.

The Vision.

ME thought I saw (as I did dreame in bed)
    A crawling Vine about *Anacreon's* head:
Flusht was his face; his haires with oyle did shine;
And as he spake, his mouth ranne ore with wine.
Tipled he was; and tipling lispt withall;
And lisping reeld, and reeling like to fall.
A young *Enchantresse* close by him did stand
Tapping his plump thighes with a *mirtle* wand:
She smil'd; he kist; and kissing, cull'd[5] her too;
And being cup-shot,[6] more he co'd not doe.
For which (me thought) in prittie anger she
Snatcht off his Crown, and gave the wreath to me:
Since when (me thinks) my braines about doe swim,
And I am wilde and wanton like to him.

A Vow to Venus.

HAPPILY I had a sight
    Of my dearest deare last night;
Make her this day smile on me,
And Ile Roses give to thee.

---

[5] =embraced.   [6] As we speak of a gun-shot wound, so a reeling tipsy, more or less helpless man, was said to be 'cup-shot.' Halliwell gives 'cap-shotten.'

On his Booke.

THE bound (almost) now of my book I see,
    But yet no end of those therein or me :
Here we begin new life ; while thousands quite
Are lost, and theirs, in everlasting night.

A Sonnet of Perilla.

THEN did I live when I did see
    Perilla smile on none but me.
But (ah !) by starres malignant crost,
The life I got I quickly lost :
But yet a way there doth remaine,
For me embalm'd to live againe ;
And that's to love me ; in which state
Ile live as one *Regenerate*.

Bad may be better.

MAN may at first transgress, but next do well :
    Vice doth in some but lodge awhile, not dwell.

Posting to Printing.

LET others to the Printing Presse run fast,
    Since after death comes glory, *Ile not haste.*

Rapine brings Ruine.

WHAT'S got by Justice is establisht sure ;
    No Kingdomes got by Rapine long endure.

Comfort to a youth that had lost his Love.

WHAT needs complaints,
    When she a place
Has with the race
    Of Saints?
In endlesse mirth,
She thinks not on
What's said or done
    In earth:
She sees no teares,
Or any tone
Of thy deep grone
    She heares:
Nor do's she minde,
Or think on't now,
That ever thou
    Wast kind.
But chang'd above,
She likes not there,
As she did here,
    Thy Love.
Forbeare therefore,
And lull asleepe
Thy woes, and weep
    No more.

Upon Boreman. *Epig.*

BOREMAN takes tole, cheats, flatters, lyes; yet *Boreman*,
For all the Divell helps, will be a poore man.

Saint Distaffs day, or the morrow after Twelth day.[7]

PARTLY worke and partly play
  Ye must on S. *Distaffs* day:
From the Plough soone free your teame;
Then come home and fother[8] them.
If the Maides a-spinning goe,
Burne the flax, and fire the tow:
Scorch their plackets,[9] but beware
That ye singe no maiden-haire.
Bring in pailes of water then,
Let the Maides bewash the men.

---

[7] I have not hitherto met with any record of this saint, nor was I aware that such ever occurred in our calendar . . . . . . St. Distaff is perhaps only a coinage of our poets, to designate the day, when the Christmas vacation being over, good housewives, with others, resumed their usual employment. N. Good Dr. Nott is perhaps too absurdly matter-of-fact. Probably St. Distaff was a piece of rustic witticism.   [8] = fodder.

[9] = a woman's pocket.

Give S. *Distaffe* all the right,
Then bid Christmas sport *good night*;
And next morrow, every one
To his owne vocation.

Sufferance.

IN the hope of ease to come,
   Let's endure one Martyrdome.

His teares to Thamasis.

I SEND, I send here my supremest kiss
   To thee, my *silver-footed Thamasis*.
No more shall I reiterate [10] thy Strand,
Whereon so many Stately Structures stand:
Nor in the summers sweeter evenings go,
To bath in thee (as thousand others doe,)
No more shall I along thy christall glide,
In Barge (with boughes and rushes beautifi'd)
With soft-smooth Virgins (for our chast disport)
To *Richmond, Kingstone,* and to *Hampton-Court*.
Never againe shall I with Finnie-Ore
Put from, or draw unto the faithfull shore:
And Landing here, or safely Landing there,
Make way to my *Beloved Westminster:*

---

[10] = pace and repace.

Or to the *Golden-cheap-side*, where the earth
Of *Julia Herrick* gave to me my Birth.
May all clean *Nimphs* and curious water Dames,
With Swan-like-state, flote up & down thy streams:
No drought upon thy wanton waters fall
To make them Leane, and languishing at all.
No ruffling winds come hither to discease [1]
Thy pure, and *Silver-wristed Naides*.
Keep up your state, ye streams; and as ye spring,
Never make sick your Banks by surfeiting.
Grow young with Tydes, and though I see ye never,
Receive this vow, *so fare-ye-well for ever.*[2]

Pardons.

THOSE ends in War the best contentment bring,
    Whose Peace is made up with a Pardoning.

Peace not Permanent.

GREAT Cities seldome rest: If there be none
    T'invade from far; They'l finde worse foes at home.

---

[1] =dis-ease, trouble or bring unrest. See Glossarial Index s. v.
[2] See Memorial-Introduction on this poem.

Truth and Errour.
TWIXT Truth and Errour, there's this difference known,
Errour is fruitfull,[3] Truth is onely one.

Things mortall, still mutable.
THINGS are uncertain, and the more we get,
The more on ycie pavements we are set.

Studies to be supported.
STUDIES themselves will languish and decay,
When either price, or praise is ta'ne away.

Wit punisht, prospers most.
DREAD not the shackles: on with thine intent;
Good wits get more fame by their punishment.

Twelfe night, or King *and* Queene.
NOW, now the mirth comes
  With the cake full of plums,
Where Beane's the *King* of the sport here;
  Beside we must know,
  The Pea also
Must revell, as *Queene,* in the Court here.

---

[3] = manifold, infinite. Plato and Cicero.

Begin then to chuse,
(This night as ye use)
Who shall for the present delight here,
Be a *King* by the lot,
And who shall not
Be Twelfe-day *Queene* for the night here.

Which knowne, let us make
Joy-sops [4] with the cake;
And let not a man then be seen here,
Who unurg'd will not drinke
To the base from the brink
A health to the King and the Queene here.

Next crowne the bowle full
With gentle lambs-wooll; [5]
Adde sugar, nutmeg, and ginger,
With store of ale too;
And thus ye must doe
To make the wassaile a swinger.[6]

Give then to the King
And Queene wassailing:
And though with ale ye be whet here;

---

[4] = sops-of-joy.
[5] See the "Oxford Night-Cap" for a receipt for this drink mixture and Glossarial Index s. v. [6] = large and full.

Yet part ye from hence,
As free from offence,
As when ye innocent met here.

His desire.

GIVE me a man that is not dull,
  When all the world with rifts[7] is full:
But unamaz'd dares clearely sing,
  Whenas the roof's a-tottering:
And, though it falls, continues still
Tickling the *Citterne*[8] with his quill.

Caution in Councell.

KNOW when to speake; for many times it brings
  Danger, to give the best advice to Kings.

Moderation.

LET moderation on thy passions waite
  Who loves too much, too much the lov'd will hate.

Advice the best actor.

STILL take advice; though counsels, when they flye
At randome, sometimes hit most happily.

---

[7] = rents. [8] = musical stringed instrument.

Conformity is comely.
CONFORMITY *gives comelinesse to things:*
And equall shares exclude all murmerings.

Lawes.
WHO violates the Customes, hurts the Health,
    Not of one man, but all the Common-wealth.

The meane.[9]
TIS much among the filthy to be clean;
    Our heat of youth can hardly keep the mean.

Like loves his like.
LIKE will to like,[1] each Creature loves his kinde;
    Chaste words proceed still from a bashfull minde.

His Hope or sheat-Anchor.
AMONG these Tempests great and manifold
    My Ship has here one only Anchor-hold;
That is my hope; which if that slip, I'm one
Wildred in this vast watry *Region*.

---

[9] = middle or medium. See Glossarial Index s. v.
[1] ὅμοιον ὁμοίῳ φίλον—a common-place of the Classics.

Comfort in Calamity.[2]

TIS no discomfort in the world to fall,
    When the great Crack[3] not Crushes one, but all.

Twilight.

THE Twi-light is no other thing (we say)
    Then Night now gone, and yet not sprung the Day.[4]

False Mourning.

HE who wears Blacks, and mournes not for the Dead,
Do's but deride the Party burièd.

The will makes the work, or consent makes the Cure.

NO grief is grown so desperate, but the ill
    Is halfe way curèd, if the party will.

Diet.

IF wholsome Diet can re-cure[5] a man,
    What need of Physick, or Physitian?

---

[2] "Solamen misseris socios habuisse dolorum."
[3] So the 'crack of Doom.'   [4] See Glossarial Index s. v.
[5] Used (then) in one sense of cure.

Smart.

STRIPES justly given yerk[6] us (with their fall)
But causelesse whipping smarts the most of all.

The Tinkers Song.

ALONG, come along,
   Let's meet in a throng
      Here of Tinkers ;
And quaffe up a Bowle
As big as a Cowle
      To Beer Drinkers.
The pole of the Hop
Place in the Ale-shop
      To Bethwack us ;
If ever we think
So much as to drink
      Unto *Bacchus.*
Who frolick will be,
For little cost he
      Must not vary,
From Beer-broth at all,
So much as to call
      For Canary.[7]

[6] Yark, yerk, jerk, jirk = to lash or whip. Here the meaning is either to hurt as lashes do, or (more probably) make us kick as does a horse under the lash. [7] Wine so named, from the Canary Isles.

His Comfort.

THE only comfort of my life
   Is, that I never yet had wife ;
Nor will hereafter ; since I know
Who Weds, ore-buyes his weal with woe.

Sincerity.

WASH clean the Vessell, lest ye soure
   Whatever Liquor in ye powre.[8]

To Anthea.

SICK is *Anthea*, sickly is the spring,
   The Primrose sick, and sickly every thing :
The while my deer *Anthea* do's but droop,
The *Tulips, Lillies, Daffadills* do *stoop ;*
But when again sh'as got her healthfull houre,
Each bending then, will rise a proper flower.

Nor buying or selling.

NOW, if you love me, tell me,
   For as I will not sell ye,
So not one cross to buy thee
Ile give, if thou deny me.

---

[8] "Sincerum est nisi vas, quodcunque infundis, acesit." Horace, Epist. i. 2, 54.

To his peculiar friend M. Jo: Wicks.[9]

SINCE shed or Cottage I have none,
　　I sing the more, that thou hast one ;
To whose glad threshold, and free door
I may a Poet come, though poor ;
And eat with thee a savory bit,
Paying but common thanks for it.
Yet sho'd I chance, (my *Wicks*) to see
An over-leven[1]-looke in thee,
To soure the Bread, and turn the Beer
To an exalted vineger ;
Or sho'dst thou prize me as a Dish
Of thrice-boyl'd-worts,[2] or third dayes fish ;
I'de rather hungry go and come,
Then to thy house be Burdensome ;　　　[*than*
Yet, in my depth of grief, I'de be
One that sho'd drop his *Beads* for thee.

The more mighty, the more mercifull.
WHO may do most, do's least : The bravest will
　　Shew mercy there, where they have power to kill.

[9] See Glossarial Index s. v.
[1] =sour, as barm or flour leavened with it, when it passes into the further stage of acetous or vinegary fermentation.
[2] =cabbage.

After Autumne, Winter.

DIE ere long, I'm sure, I shall;
   After leaves, the tree must fall.

A good death.

FOR truth I may this sentence tell,
   No man dies ill, that liveth well.[3]

Recompence.

WHO plants an Olive, but to eate the Oile?
   Reward, we know, is the chiefe end of toile.

On Fortune.

THIS is my comfort, when she's most unkind,
   She can but spoile me of my Meanes, not Mind.

To Sir George Parrie, Doctor of the Civill Law.[4]

I HAVE my Laurel Chaplet on my head,
   If 'mongst these many Numbers to be read,
But one by you be hug'd and cherishèd.

---

[3] See Memorial-Introduction for parallel later (in Pope).

[4] He was admitted to the College of Advocates, London, 3rd Nov., 1628; but almost nothing has been transmitted concerning him save that he married the d. and heir of Sir Giles Sweet, Dean of Arches.

Peruse my Measures thoroughly, and where
Your judgement finds a guilty Poem, there
Be you a Judge; but not a Judge severe.

The meane passe by, or over, none contemne;
The good applaud: the peccant lesse condemne,
Since *Absolution* you can give to them.

Stand forth Brave Man, here to the publique sight;
And in my Booke now claim a two-fold right:
The first as *Doctor*, and the last as *Knight*.

Charmes.

THIS Ile tell ye by the way,
    Maidens when ye Leavens[5] lay,
Crosse your Dow,[6] and your dispatch,
Will be better for your Batch.[7]

Another.[8]

IN the morning when ye rise,
    Wash your hands, and cleanse your eyes.
Next be sure ye have a care,
To disperse the water farre.

---

[5] Also 'leavance'—the dough mingled with the barm or leavened: and though to lay leavance is explained by some as to mingle the two, it is more probably to lay it aside to rise or leaven.

[6] = dough.   [7] = the baking, or quantity or number baked.

[8] and [9] Folk-lore.

For as farre as that doth light,
So farre keepes the evill Spright.[9]

Another.

IF ye feare to be affrighted
   When ye are (by chance) benighted :
In your Pocket for a trust,
Carrie nothing but a Crust :
For that holy piece of Bread
Charmes the danger, and the dread.

Upon Gorgonius.[1]

UNTO *Pastillus* ranke *Gorgonius* came,
   To have a tooth twitcht out of's native frame.
Drawn was his tooth; but stanke so, that some say,
The Barber stopt his Nose, and ranne away.

Gentlenesse.

THAT Prince must govern with a gentle hand,
   Who will have love comply with his command.

---

[1] There is a slip here in the names: no doubt Herrick was thinking of Horace, Sat. i. 4, 92 : "Pastillos Rufillus olet, Gorgonius hircum," and has made Pastillos into a man.

A Dialogue betwixt himselfe and Mistresse Eliza:
Wheeler, *under the name of* Amarillis.[2]

    MY dearest Love, since thou wilt go,
        And leave me here behind thee;
    For love or pitie let me know
        The place where I may find thee.

Amaril. In country Meadowes pearl'd with Dew,
        And set about with Lillies;
    There filling Maunds[3] with Cowslips, you
        May find your *Amarillis*.

Her. What have the Meades to do with thee,
        Or with thy youthfull houres?
    Live thou at Court, where thou mayst be
        The *Queen* of men, not flowers.

    Let Country wenches make 'em fine
        With Poesies,[4] since 'tis fitter
    For thee with richest Jemmes to shine,
        And like the Starres to glitter.

Amaril. You set too high a rate upon
        A Shepheardess so homely;
Her. Believe it (dearest) ther's not one
        I'th' Court that's halfe so comly.

---

[2] See Glossarial Index s. v.
[3] = baskets. See Glossarial Index s. v.   [4] = posies.

  I prithee stay. (*Am.*) I must away;
   Lets kiss first, then we'l sever.
Ambo. And though we bid adieu to day,
   Wee shall not part for ever.

To Julia.

HELP me, *Julia*, for to pray,
 Mattens sing, or Mattens say :[5]
This I know, the Fiend will fly
Far away, if thou beest by.
Bring the Holy-water hither;
Let us wash, and pray together :
When our Beads are thus united,
Then the Foe will fly affrighted.

To Roses in Julia's *Bosome.*

ROSES, you can never die,
 Since the place wherein ye lye,
Heat and moisture mixt are so,
As to make ye ever grow.

To the Honoured, Master Endimion Porter.[6]

WHEN to thy Porch I come, and (ravisht) see
 The State of Poets there attending Thee :

---

[5] = matins.   [6] See Glossarial Index s. v.

Those *Bardes* and I, all in a *Chorus* sing,
We are Thy *Prophets Porter;* Thou our King.

Speake in season.

WHEN times are troubled, then forbeare; but
    speak,
When a cleare day, out of a Cloud do's break.

Obedience.

THE Power of Princes rests in the Consent
    Of onely those, who are obedient:
Which if away, proud Scepters then will lye
Low, and of Thrones the Ancient *Majesty.*

Another on the same.

N*O man so well a Kingdome Rules, as He,*
    Who hath himselfe obaid the Soveraignty.

Of Love.

1. INSTRUCT me now, what love will do;
2.   'Twill make a tongless man to wooe.
1. Inform me next, what love will do;
2. 'Twill strangely make a one of too.   [*two*
1. Teach me besides, what love wil do;
2. 'Twill quickly mar, & make ye too.

1. Tell me, now last, what love will do;
2. 'Twill hurt and heal a heart pierc'd through.

Upon Trap.

TRAP, of a Player turn'd a Priest now is;
    Behold a suddaine *Metamorphosis*.
If Tythe-pigs faile, then will he shift the scean,
And, from a Priest, turne Player once again.

Upon Grubs.

GRUBS loves his Wife and Children, while that they
Can live by love, or else grow fat by Play:
But when they call or cry on *Grubs* for meat;
Instead of Bread, *Grubs* gives them stones to eat.
He raves, he rends, and while he thus doth tear,
His Wife and Children fast to death for fear.

Upon Dol.

NO question but *Dols* cheeks wo'd soon rost dry,
    Were they not basted by her either eye.

Upon Hog.

HOG has a place i'th' Kitchen, and his share
    The flimsie Livers, and blew Gizzards are.

The School or Perl of Putney, *the Mistress of all singular manners, Mistresse* Portman.[7]

WHETHER I was my selfe, or else did see
    Out of my self that *Glorious Hierarchie!*
Or whether those (in orders rare) or these
Made up One State of *Sixtie Venuses;*
Or whether *Fairies, Syrens, Nymphes* they were,
Or *Muses*, on their mountaine sitting there;
Or some enchanted Place, I do not know
(Or *Sharon*, where eternall Roses grow.)
This I am sure; I Ravisht stood, as one
Confus'd in utter Admiration.
Me thought I saw them stir, and gently move,
And look as all were capable of Love:
And in their motion smelt much like to flowers
Enspir'd by th' Sun-beams after dews & showers.
There did I see the *Reverend Rectresse* stand,
Who with her eyes-gleam, or a glance of hand,
Those spirits rais'd; and with like precepts then,
(As with a *Magick*) laid them all agen:

---

[7] Mr. Henry Portman occurs frequently in the Putney Parish Register during Herrick's period, and a Mrs. Mary Portman was buried there 27th June, 1671. Apparently mistress of a finishing school of deportment.

(A happy Realme! When no compulsive Law,
Or fear of it, but Love keeps all in awe.)
Live you, *great Mistresse* of your Arts, and be
A nursing Mother so to Majesty;
As those your Ladies may in time be seene,
For Grace and Carriage, every one a Queene.
One Birth their Parents gave them; but their new,
And better Being, they receive from You.
Mans former Birth is grace-lesse; but the state
Of life comes in, when he's Regenerate.

To Perenna.

THOU say'st I'm dull; if edge-lesse so I be,
    Ile whet my lips, and sharpen Love on thee.

On himselfe.

LET me not live, if I not love,
    Since I as yet did never prove,
Where Pleasures met: at last, doe find,
All Pleasures meet in Woman-kind.

On Love.

THAT love 'twixt men do's ever longest last
    Where War and Peace the Dice by turns doe cast.

Another on Love.

LOVE'S of it self, too sweet ; the best of all
  Is, when loves hony has a dash of gall.

Upon Gut.

SCIENCE puffs up, sayes *Gut,* when either Pease
  Make him thus swell, or windy Cabbages.

Upon Chub.

WHEN *Chub* brings in his harvest, still he cries,
  Aha my boyes ! heres wheat for Christmas
    Pies !
Soone after, he for beere so scores [8] his wheat,
That at the tide, he has not bread to eate.

Pleasures Pernicious.

WHERE Pleasures rule a Kingdome, never there
  Is sober virtue seen to move her sphere.

On himself.

A WEARIED Pilgrim, I have wandred here
  Twice five and twenty (bate me but one yeer)
Long I have lasted in this world ; ('tis true)
But yet those yeers that I have liv'd, but few.

[8] = runs up a score that is to be paid by his wheat, or by the price of it.

Who by his gray Haires, doth his lusters tell,
Lives not those yeers, but he that lives them well.
One man has reatch't his sixty yeers, but he
Of all those three-score, has not liv'd halfe three : [9]
He lives, who lives to virtue : men who cast
Their ends for Pleasure, do not live, but last.

To M. Laurence Swetnaham.[1]

READ thou my Lines, my *Swetnaham*, if there be
    A fault, 'tis hid, if it be voic't by thee.
Thy mouth will make the sourest numbers please ;
How will it drop pure hony, speaking these ?

His Covenant or Protestation to Julia.

WHY do'st thou wound, & break my heart,
    As if we sho'd for ever part ?

---

[9] Cf. Randolph and Herbert. See Memorial-Introduction.

[1] Baptisms of children of Lawrence Swettenham occur in the Parish Register of St. Margaret's, Westminster, as early as 1625, and in an Act Book of the Dean and Chapter of Westminster, 10th July, 1639, *Laurence Swetnam*, Gent., is mentioned as a church-warden of St. Margaret's. Thomas Swettenham, of Swettenham, co. Chester, Esq., who married, in 1602, Mary, d. of John Birtles, of Birtles Esquire, had a third son named Lawrence. Lawrence Sweatnam was buried in the East Cloister of Westminster Abbey, 2nd May, 1673. Cf. Col. Chester's " Westminster Abbey," s. n.

Hast thou not heard an Oath from me,
After a day, or two, or three,
I wo'd come back and live with thee?
Take, if thou do'st distrust that Vowe;
This second Protestation now.
Upon thy cheeke that spangel'd Teare,
Which sits as Dew of Roses there:
That Teare shall scarce be dri'd before
Ile kisse the Threshold of thy dore.
Then weepe not, sweet; but thus much know,
I'm halfe return'd before I go.

On himselfe.

I WILL no longer kiss,
  I can no longer stay;
The way of all Flesh is,
  That I must go this day:
Since longer I can't live,
  My frolick Youths adieu;
My Lamp to you Ile give,
  And all my troubles too.

To the most accomplisht Gentleman Master Michael Oulsworth.

NOR thinke that Thou in this my Booke art worst,
  Because not plac't here with the midst, or first.

Since Fame that sides with these, or goes before
Those, that must live with Thee for evermore.
That Fame, and Fames rear'd Pillar, thou shalt see
In the next sheet, *Brave Man,* to follow Thee.
Fix on that Columne then, and never fall ;
Held up by Fames *eternall Pedestall.*

To his Girles who would have him sportfull.

ALAS! I can't, for tell me how
    Can I be gamesome (agèd now :)
Besides, ye see me daily grow
Here, Winter-like, to Frost and Snow.
And I ere long, my Girles, shall see,
Ye quake for cold to looke on me.

Truth and falsehood.
TRUTH by her own simplicity is known ;
    Falsehood by Varnish and Vermillion.

His last request to Julia.

I HAVE been wanton, and too bold I feare,
    To chafe o'remuch the Virgins cheek or eare :
Beg for my Pardon, *Julia ; He doth winne*
Grace with the Gods, who's sorry for his sinne.
That done, my *Julia,* dearest *Julia,* come,
And go with me to chuse my Buriall roome :

My Fates are ended; when thy *Herrick* dyes,
Claspe thou his Book, then close thou up his Eyes.

On himselfe.

ONE Eare tingles;[2] some there be,
   That are snarling now at me:
Be they those that *Homer* bit,
I will give them thanks for it.

Upon Kings.

KINGS must be dauntlesse: Subjects will contemne
   Those, who want Hearts, and weare a Diadem.

To his Girles.

WANTON Wenches doe not bring
   For my haires black colouring:
For my Locks (Girles) let 'em be
Gray or white, all's one to me.

Upon Spur.

SPUR jingles now, and sweares by no meane oathes,
He's double honour'd, since h'as got gay cloathes:

---

[2] There seems to be a reference here to the classical notion, as in Virgil: Bucol. It is of still living folk-lore.

Most like his Suite, and all commend the Trim;
And thus they praise the Sumpter; but not him:
As to the Goddesse, people did conferre
Worship, and not to'th' Asse that carried her.[3]

To his Brother Nicolas Herrick.[4]

WHAT others have with cheapnesse seene, and ease,
In Varnisht Maps; by'th' helpe of Compasses:
Or reade in Volumes, and those Bookes (with all
Their large Narrations, *Incanonicall*)[5]
Thou hast beheld those seas, and Countries farre;
And tel'st to us, what once they were, and are.
So that with bold truth, thou canst now relate
This Kingdomes fortune, and that Empires fate:
Canst talke to us of *Sharon;* where a spring
Of Roses have an endlesse flourishing.
Of *Sion, Sinai, Nebo,* and with them,
Make knowne to us the new *Jerusalem.*
The Mount of *Olives; Calverie,* and where
Is (and hast seene) thy *Saviours Sepulcher.*

---

[3] = the ass carrying the mysteries: cf. Aristophanes' Frogs, 159.
[4] See Memorial-Introduction.
[5] = un-canonical, and therefore not to be wholly relied on.

So that the man that will but lay his eares,
As *Inapostate*,[6] to the thing he heares,
Shall by his hearing quickly come to see
The truth of Travails lesse in bookes then Thee.
[*than*

The Voice and Violl.

RARE is the voice itselfe; but when we sing
  To'th' Lute or Violl, then 'tis ravishing.

Warre.

IF Kings and kingdomes, once distracted be,
  The sword of war must trie the Soveraignty.

A King and no King.

THAT Prince, who may doe nothing but what's just,
  Rules but by leave, and takes his Crowne on trust.

Plots not still prosperous.

ALL are not ill Plots, that doe sometimes faile;
  Nor those false vows, which oft times don't
    prevaile.

---

[6] = a non-apostate—one who does not revolt or turn away. In next line 'by' is misprinted 'be.'

Flatterie.

WHAT is't that wasts a Prince? example showes,
'Tis flatterie spends a King, more then his foes. [*than*

Upon Rumpe.

RUMPE is a Turne-broach,[7] yet he seldome can
    Steale a swolne sop out of the Dripping pan.

Upon Shopter.

OLD Widow *Shopter*, whensoere she cryes,
    Lets drip a certain Gravie from her eyes.

Upon Deb.

IF felt and heard, (unseen) thou dost me please;
    If seen, thou lik'st me, *Deb*, in none of these.

Excesse.

EXCESSE is sluttish: keepe the meane; for why?
    Vertue's clean Conclave is sobriety.

Upon Croot.

ONE silver spoon shines in the house of *Croot*;
    Who cannot buie, or steale a second to't.

---

[7] = turn-spit.

The Soul is the salt.

THE body's salt, the soule is; which when gon,
The flesh soone sucks in putrifaction.

Upon Flood, or a thankfull man.

FLOOD, if he has for him and his a bit,
   He sayes his fore and after Grace for it:
If meate he wants, then Grace he sayes to see
His hungry belly borne by Legs *Jaile-free*.
Thus have, or have not, all alike is good,
To this our poore, yet ever patient *Flood*.

Upon Pimpe.

WHEN *Pimpes* feet sweat (as they doe often use)
   There springs a sope-like-lather in his shoos.

Upon Luske.

IN Den'-shire Kerzie *Lusk* [8] (when he was dead)
   Wo'd shrouded be, and therewith buried.
When his Assignes askt him the reason why?
He said, because he got his wealth thereby.

Foolishnesse.

IN'S *Tusc'lanes*, *Tullie* doth confesse,
   No plague ther's like to foolishnesse.

[8] Devonshire was in former times famous for manufactures.

Upon Rush.

RUSH saves his shooes, in wet and snowie wether;
   And feares in summer to weare out the lether:
This is strong thrift that warie *Rush* doth use
Summer and Winter still to save his shooes.

Abstinence.

AGAINST diseases here the strongest fence
   Is the defensive vertue, Abstinence.

No danger to men desperate.

WHEN feare admits no hope of safety, then
   Necessity makes dastards valiant men.

Sauce for sorrowes.

ALTHOUGH our suffering meet with no reliefe,
   An equall mind is the best sauce for griefe.[1]

To Cupid.

I HAVE a leaden, thou a shaft of gold;
   Thou kil'st with heate, and I strike dead with cold.

---

[1] "Æquam memento rebus in arduis
   Servare mentem," &c. Horace, Od. II. iii. ll. 1—2.

Let's trie of us who shall the first expire ;
Or thou by frost, or I by quenchlesse fire :
Extreames are fatall, where they once doe strike.
And bring to'th' heart destruction both alike.

Distrust.

WAT ever men for Loyalty pretend,
   Tis Wisdomes part to doubt a faithfull friend.[2]

The Hagg.

THE staffe is now greas'd :
   And very well pleas'd,
She cockes out her Arse at the parting,
   To an old Ram Goat,
   That rattles i'th' throat,
Halfe choakt with the stink of her farting.

   In a dirtie Haire-lace
   She leads on a brace
Of black-bore-cats[3] to attend her ;
   Who scratch at the Moone,
   And threaten at noone
Of night from Heaven for to rend her.

---

[2] From Aristotle onward, this has been a common-place.
[3] = male cats.

A-hunting she goes;
A crackt horne she blowes;
At which the hounds fall a-bounding;
While th' Moone in her sphere
Peepes trembling for feare,
And night's afraid of the sounding.

The mount of the Muses.

AFTER thy labour take thine ease,
Here with the sweet *Pierides*.
But if so be that men will not
Give thee the Laurell Crowne for lot;
Be yet assur'd, thou shalt have one
Not subject to corruption.

On Himselfe.

ILE write no more of Love; but now repent
Of all those times that I in it have spent.
Ile write no more of life; but wish 'twas ended,
And that my dust was to the earth commended.

To his Booke.

GOE thou forth, my booke, though late;
Yet be timely fortunate.

It may chance good-luck may send
Thee a kinsman, or a friend,
That may harbour thee, when I,
With my fates neglected lye.
If thou know'st not where to dwell,
See, the fier's by : *Farewell.*

The end of his worke.

PART of the worke remaines ; one part is past :
And here my ship rides having Anchor cast.

To Crowne it.

MY wearied Barke, O let it now be Crown'd !
The Haven reacht to which I first was bound.

On Himselfe.

THE worke is done : young men and maidens, set
Upon my curles the *Mirtle Coronet,*
Washt with sweet ointments ; Thus at last I come
To suffer in the Muses *Martyrdome:*
But with this comfort, if my blood be shed,
The Muses will weare blackes, when I am dead.

The pillar of Fame.

FAMES pillar here, at last, we set,
 Out-during[4] *Marble*, *Brasse*, or *Jet*,
  Charm'd and enchanted so,
  As to withstand the blow,
   Of overthrow,
   Nor shall the seas,
   Or OUTRAGES
  Of storms orebear
  What we up-rear :
  Tho Kingdoms fal,
 This pillar never shall
 Decline or waste at all;
But stand for ever by his owne
Firme and well - fixt foundation.[5]

TO his Book's end this last line he'd have plac't,
 Jocond his Muse was; but his *Life* was chast.[6]

FINIS.

[4] = out-lasting.

[5] Horatian to the last is the bard Robert Herrick, concluding what he terms his *Works Human* with an imitation of
  Exegi monumentum ære perennius, &c.
    Horat. Ode ult. Lib. 3. N.

[6] On this couplet see Cartwright's stinging allusion in our Memorial-Introduction.

NOTE.

The following Poems are gathered as so many fallen 'Golden Apples' of the Hesperides: hence my title. The source of each is given in its place. To Mr. W. C. Hazlitt belongs the credit of having been the first to print or reprint the whole of these save the last (Vol. II. pp. 433-447); but the first, "The Description of a Woman," is taken from "Wit's Recreations" (1640), with additions and corrections from the Ashmole MS. 38, page 88, Art. 109 (viz. ll. 47-50, 57-8, 63-76, 79-84, 103-4, 109-112, and ll. 15-16 ('shew' and 'growe' for 'shown' and 'grown.'). A collation of the Ashmole MSS. and of the original books has corrected a great number of faulty readings, as well as given accurate references to the several places in the MSS. One poem (III) demanded very careful revision, being a mass of errors. On these Poems see our Memorial-Introduction, where it will be seen they are all-important biographically. The various readings of I. are also therein critically examined, along with others. Prefixed to it is a fac-simile of 'the Woman' from 'Wit's Recreations.' Instead of the "6 or 8" mentioned by Mr. Hazlitt, it will be seen in our Memorial-Introduction that no fewer than 62 of the poems of "Hesperides" appeared originally in "Wit's Recreations," exclusive of "The Description of a Woman." All this has hitherto been strangely overlooked by the Editors of Herrick and Bibliographers, and equally so that herein first appeared some of the choice poems of Crashaw, Milton, &c., &c. G.

GOLDEN APPLES.

I. *The Discription of a Woman.*[1]

WHOSE head befringèd with be-scatterèd tresses,
Shews like *Apolloes*, when the morn he dresses:

[1] From "Wit's Recreations" (1640) as in Note on page 90 and Ashmole M.S. 38, page 88, Art. 109.

Or like *Aurora* when with Pearle she sets
Her long disheveld Rose-crown'd Trammelets:[2]
Her forehead smooth, full polish'd, bright and high,
Bears in itself a gracefull Majesty;
Under the which, two crawling eye-brows twine
Like to the tendrills of a flatt'ring Vine:
Under whose shade, two starry sparkling eyes
Are beautifi'd with faire fringd Canopies.   10
Her comely nose with uniformall grace,
Like purest white, stands in the middle place,
Parting the paire, as wee may well suppose,
Each cheek resembling still a damaske Rose:
Which like a Garden manifestlye shew
How Roses, Lillies, and Carnations growe;
Which sweetly mixèd both with white and red,
Like Rose leaves, white and redd, seem minglèd.
Then nature, for a sweet allurement sets
Two smelling, swelling, bashfull Cherrylets;[3]   20
The which with ruby-rednesse being tip'd,
Do speake a Virgin, merry, Cherry-lip'd.
Over the which a neat sweet skin is drawne,
Which makes them shew like Roses under Lawne;

---

[2] = nets for the hair. See Glossarial Index s. v.
[3] = diminutive of cherries.

These be the Ruby-portals, and divine,
Which ope themselues, to shew a holy shrine,
Whose breath is rich perfume, that to the sense
Smells like the burn'd *Sabean* Frankinsense;
In which the tongue, though but a member small,
Stands guarded with a Rosie-hilly-wall; 30
And her white teeth, which in her gums are set,
Like Pearl and Gold, make one rich Cabinet.
Next doth her chin, with dimpled beauty strive
For his white, plump, and smooth, prerogative;
At whose faire top, to please the sight there grows
The fairest image of a blushing rose;
Mou'd by the chin, whose motion causeth this,
That both her lips do part, do meet, do kiss,
Her ears, which like two labyrinths are plac'd
On eyther side, with rich rare Jewels grac'd: 40
Mouing a question, whether that by them,
The Jem is grac'd, or they grac'd by the Jem.
But the foundation of the Architect
Is the Swan-staining, faire, rare, stately neck,
Which with ambitious humblenesse stands under,
Bearing aloft this rich-round world of wounder.
Jn which the veynes jmplanted, seeme to lye
Lyke louing vines hidde vnder juorie;
So full of clarrett, that whosoe prickes this vine
May see itt sprout forth streames lyke Muskadine. 50

Her breast, a place for beauties throne most fit,
Bears up two Globes, where love and pleasure sitt;
Which, headed with two rich round Rubies, show
Like wanton Rose-buds growing out of Snow,
And in the milky valley that's between,
Sits *Cupid*, kissing of his mother Queen:
Ffingering the papps that feele like sleuèd[5] silke,
And prest a little, thay will weep pewr milke.
Then comes the belly, seated next below,
Like a faire mountain of *Riphean* snow;   60
Whear Nature, in a whitenesse without spot,
Hath in the middle tide a Gordian knott;
Or else that she in that white waxen hill
Hath seald the primrose[6] of her vttmost skill;
But now my muse hath spied a darke descent
Ffrom this soe pretious pearly permanent,[7]
A milkye highe-way that direction yelds
Vnto the port-mouth of the Elizean feilds:
A place desired of all, but gott by these
Whom loue admitts to the Hesperides;   70
Hers, goulden fruitt, that doth excede all price
Growing in this Loue-guarded parradice;
Aboue the entrance, theire is wrighten this,
This is the portail to the bower of blisse,

[5] Soft changeable-coloured silk.
[6] See Glossarial Index s. v.   [7] Qu.—pavement?

GOLDEN APPLES. 95

Through mid'st whearof, a christall streame there
    flowes
Passing the sweete-sweete of a muskie rose.
Now Loue invites me to survey hur thighes,
Swelling in likenesse like to Crystall skyes,
With plump softe flesh, of mettall pure and fine,
Resembling sheildes, both pure and christaline.   80
Hence rise those two ambitious hills, that looke
Jnto ye middle sweet sight-stealing crooke,
Which for the better bewtifing shrowds
Its humble selfe 'twixt two aspiring cloudes;
Which to the knees by nature fastned on,
Deriue their ever well 'greed motion.
Her legs with two clear calves, like siluer try'd,
Kindly swell up, with little pretty pride,
Leaving a distance for the comely small
To beautifie the leg and foot withall.   90
Then lowly, yet most lovely stand the feet,
Round, short and clear, lyke pounded Spices sweet;
And whatsoever thing they tread upon
They make it scent like bruisèd Cinnamon.
The lovely shoulders now allure the eye,
To see two Tablets of pure ivorie:
From which two arms like branches seem to spread,
With tender vein'd and siluer colouerèd;

With little hands and fingers long and small,
To grace a Lute, a Violl, Virginall.   100
In length each finger doth his next excell,
Each richly headed with a pearly shell;
Richer then that fayre, pretious, vertuous horne[8] [*than*
That armes the forehead of the unicorne.
Thus euery parte in contrariety
Meet in the whole and make an harmony;
As divers strings do singly disagree,
But form'd by Number, make sweet melodie.
Vnto the jdoll of the worke deuine
J consecrate this louing life of myne,   110
Bowing my lipps vnto that stately roote
Wheare bewtye springs; and thus j kiss (her) foote.[9]

II. *Mr. Hericke his Daughters Dowrye.*[1]

ERE J goe hence and bee noe more
   Seene to the world, J'le giue the skore
J owe vnto a female child,
And that is this, a uerse jnstylde

---

[8] The horn of the (mythical) unicorn was endowed with mystic curative virtues.

[9] = The MS. is signed " Finis. Robt. Herrick."   [1] From the Ashmole MS. 38, p. 94, Art. 112.

GOLDEN APPLES. 97

My daughters dowrye; haueing which,
J'le leaue thee then compleatly riche;
Jnsteade of gould, pearle, rubies, bonds,
Longe forfaite pawnèd diamonds,
Or antique pledges, house or lande;
J giue thee this that shall withstande   10
The blow of ruine and of chance:
Theis hurte not thyne jnheritance,
For 'tis ffee simple, and noe rent
Thou fortune ow'st for tenement;
Howeuer after tymes will praise,
This portion, my prophetique bayes,
Cannot deliuer vpp to th' rust,
Yet J keepe peacefull in my dust.
As for thy birth, and better seeds
(Those which must growe to vertuous deeds: 20
Thou didst deriue from that old steem [2]
Loue and Mercie, cherish them),
Which, like a vestall virgine ply
With holye fier, least that itt dye.
Growe vpp with mylder lawes[3] to knowe
Att what tyme to say I[4] or noe;

---

[2] = stem: I have placed l. 21 before l. 20 of the MS., which is here evidently in error.   [3] i. e. under milder laws than those of the vestals.   [4] = ay.

Lett manners teach thee whear to bee
More comely flowing, where les free :
Theis bringe thy husband, like to those
Old coynes and meddalls wee expose   30
To th' shew, but neuer part with ; next
As jn a more conspicuous text,
(Thy forehead) lett therin bee sign'd
The mayden candour [5] of thy mynde ;
And vnder it two chast-borne spyes
To barr out bolde adulteryes :
Ffor through these optickes, fly the dartes
Of lust, which sette on fier our hartes.
On eyther side of theis, quicke eares
Ther must bee plac'd, for seasoned feares, 40
Which sweeten loue, yett ne're come nighe
The plague of wilder jelousie.
Then lett each cheeke of thyne, intice
His soule as to a bedd of spice ;
Wheare hee may roule, and loose his sence
As in a bedd of frankensence :
A lipp jnkyndlèd with that coale,
With which Loue chafes and warmes the soule,
Bringe to hym next,[6] and in it shew
Loues cherries ; from such fyers growe   50

[5] whiteness, purity.
[6] The construction is 'Bring to him next a lip' . . . .

And haue their haruest, which must stand
The gathering of the lipp, not hand;
Then vnto theis, bee it thy care
To cloath thy words in gentle ayre,
That smooth as oyle, sweet, softe and cleane
As is the childish [7] bloome of beane,
They may fall downe and stroake (as the
Beames of the sunn the gracefull sea):
With handes as smooth as mercies, bring
Hym for his better cherrishing.[8] 60
That when thou doest his necke jnsnare,
Or with thy wrist, or fluttering hayre,
Hee may (a prisoner) ther discrye
Bondage more loued then lybertye; [than
A nature, soe well form'd, soe wrought,
To [9] calme and tempest, lett bee brought
With thee, that should hee but jnclyne
To roughnes, claspe hym lyke a vine;
Or lyke as woole meetes steele, giue way
Vnto the passion, not to stay;[1] 70
Wrath yf resisted ouer-boyles,
Jff not, it dyes, or eles recoyles;

[7] = just sprouting.
[8] There seems some omission after this, and also, judging from the confusion, after 'sea' preceding.
[9] Miswritten 'Too.'   [1] i. e. do not attempt to oppose its stay.

And lastly, see you bring to hym,
Somewhat peculiar to each lymm;
And j charge thee to bee knowne
By n' other face, but by thyne owne.
Lett itt (in Loues name) bee keept sleeke
Yett to bee found when hee shall seeke
Jt, and not jnstead of [to] saint,
Giue vpp his worth vnto the painte; 80
Ffor (trust me girle) shee ouer-does
Who by a double proxie woes;
But least j should forgett his bedd,
Bee sure thou bringe a mayden-head,
That is a Margarite,[2] which lost,
Thou bring'st vnto his bedd a frost
Or a colde poyson, which his blood
Benummes like the forgettfull [3] floode.
Now for some jewells to supplye
The wante of eare-rings brauerye, 90
Ffor publike eyes; take onlye theis,
Ne're broughte far beyonde the seas;
Theyre nobly-home-breed, yett haue price
Beyound the fare-fetch [4] marchandize.
Obedience, wise-distrust, peace, shey[5]
Distance, and sweet vrbanitie:

[2] = pearl.   [3] = of Lethe.   [4] Miswritten 'fetch.'   [5] = shy.

Safe modestie, lou'd patience, feare
Of offending, temperance, deare
Constancie, bashfullnes, and all
The vertues lesse, or cardinall,   100
Take with my blessinge; and goe forth
Jnjewelld with thy natiue worthe.
And now yf ther a man bee founde,
That lookes for such pareèd grownd,
Lett hym, but with indifferent skill,
Soe good a soile bee-stocke and till;
Hee may ere longe haue such a wyfe,
Nourish in's breast, a Tree of Life.

                 Finis.   ROBT. HERICKE.

III. *Mr. Robert Hericke his Farwell vnto Poetrie.*[6]

I HAUE behelde two louers, in a night
   Hatcht[7] o're with moone-shine, from their stolen
      delight,—
When this to that, and that to this, had giuen
A kisse to such a jewell of the heuen:

---

[6] From the Ashmole MS. 38, p. 108, Art. 121. The MS. is a chaos of mispunctuation, and it is not improved by Mr. Hazlitt. An attempt has been made to rectify wrong words, and improving punctuation. See Memorial-Introduction specially.

[7] = engraved, inlaid.

Or while that each from other's breath did drincke
Healthes to the rose, the violet, or pinke,—
Call'd [8] on the suddayne by the jealouse mother,
Some strickter Mrs. or suspitious other,
Vrging diuorcement (woorse then death to theis) [than
By the soone gingling of some sleepy keyes,
Parte with a hastye kisse; and in that shew
How stay thay would, yet forc't thay are to goe.
Euen such are wee: and in our parting, doe
Noe otherwise then as those former two;   [than
Natures like ours, wee who haue spent our tyme
Both from the morning to the euening chyme;
Nay, till [9] the bell-man [1] of the night had tould
Past noone of night, yett weare [2] the howers not old,
Nor dull'd with yron sleeps, but haue out-worne
The fresh and fayrest flourish of the morne
With flame, and rapture; drincking to the ode [3]
Number of wyne, which makes vs full with God,
And yn that misticke frenzie, wee haue hurl'de,
(As with a tempeste) nature [4] through the worlde,
And yn a whirl-wynd twirl'd her home, agast
Att that which in her extasie had past;

---

[8] The construction is Called &c. (l. 7) from their stolen delight.
[9] Miswritten 'tell.'   [1] See Glossarial Index s. v.   [2] =were.
[3] =odd.—οἶνος and *vinum* both give 5 the number of perfection.
[4] i. e. our nature, our spirit.

Thus crownd with rose-budds, sacke, thou mad'st
    mee flye
Like fier-drakes,[5] yett didst mee no harme therby.
O thou allmightye nature, who did'st giue
True heate, whearwith humanitie doth liue
Beyond its stinted [6] circle ; giueing foode
White fame,[7] and resurrection to the good ;
Soaring them vpp, boue ruyne, till the doome
The generall Aprill [8] of the worlde dothe come,
That makes all æquall. Manye thowsands should
(Wert not for thee) haue crumbled ynto mould,
And with thayr ceareclothes rotted, not to shew[9]
Whether the world such sperritts had or noe,
Whearas by thee, those, and a million since,
Nor fate, nor enuye, cann theyr fames conuince.[1]
Homer, Musæus, Ouid, Maro, more,
Of those god-full prophetts longe before
Helde [2] there [3] eternall fiers ; and ours of late
(Thy mercie helping) shall resist stronge fate,
Nor stoope to th' center, but suruiue as longe
As fame or rumour, hath or trumpe or tongue ;

  [5] The ignis fatuus (plural).
  [6] = stopped, i.e. confined.   [7] See Glossarial Index s. v. = good or happy, fame.   [8] See Glossarial Index s. v.   [9] = so as not (or never) to shew.   [1] = overcome.
  [2] Miswritten 'Holde.'   [3] = their.

But vnto mee, bee onlye hoarse, since now
(Heauen and my soule beare record of my vowe)
I, my desires screw from thee, and directe
Them and my thoughts to that sublim'd respecte
And conscience vnto priesthood ; tis not need
(The skarcrow vnto mankinde) that doth breed
Wiser conclusions in mee, since I knowe
I've more to beare my chardges,[4] then way to goe; [*than*
Or had I not, I'de stopp the spreading itch
Off craueing more : soe yn conceipt bee ritch ;   [*of*
But tis the god of nature who yntends,
And shaps my function for more glorious ends :
Kisse,[5] soe departe; yett stay awhile to [6] see
The lines of sorrowe, that lye drawne in mee
Yn speach, in picture ; noe otherwise then when, [*than*
(Judgment and death, denounc'd gainst guilty men),
Each takes a weeping farewell, rackt in mynde
With joyes before, and pleasures left behind :
Shakeing the head, whilst each to each dothe mourne
With thought thay goe, whence thay must ner
    returne.
Soe with like lookes, as once the ministrell
Cast, leading his Euredice through hell,

---

[4] Miswritten ' I am ..... chardge :'=I have more [money] to bear my chardges than I have road to travel.   [5] Miswritten 'Guesse.'   [6] Again miswritten ' too.'

I stricke thy loues, and greedyly persue
Thee, with myne eyes, or in, or out, of view.
Soe look't the Grecian oratour when sent
Ffroms natiue cuntrye, into banishment,
Throwing his eye-balls backward to suruaye
The smoake of his beloued Attica :[7]
Soe Tullye [8] look't, when from the brooks of Rome
The sad soule went, not with his loue, but doome :
Shooting his eye-darts 'gainst it, to surprise
Yt, or to drawe the cittie to his eyes.
Such is my parting with thee; and to proue
Ther was not varnish (only) in my loue,
But substance, lo! receaue this pearlye teare
Ffrozen with greife, and place it in thyne eare,
Then parte in name of peace; and softely on
With numerous [9] feete to Hoofy [1] Helicon;
And when thou art vppon that sacred hill
Amongest the thrice three sacred virgins, fill
A full brimm'd bowle of furye and of rage,
And quafe it to the prophets of our age;
When drunck with rapture, curse the blind and lame
Base ballad-mongers, who vsurpe thy name
And fowle thy altar; charme some ynto froggs,
Some to bee ratts, and others to bee hoggs;

[7] Demosthenes.   [8] Cicero.
[9] =rythmical.   [1] =alluding to Pegasus.

Ynto the loathsoms ['t] shapps thou canst deuise
To make ffooles hate them, onlye by disguise;
Thus with a kisse of warmth, and loue, I parte
Not soe, but that some relique yn my harte
Shall stand for euer, though I doe addresse
Chiefelye my selfe to what I must proffess:
Knowe yet (rare soule) when my diuiner muse
Shall want a hand-mayde (as she ofte will vse),[2]
Bee readye, thou for mee, to wayte vppon her,
Thoughe as a seruant, yet a mayde of honor.
The crowne of dutye is our dutye: well
Doing's, the fruite of doinge well.   Farewell.
     Fimis.   MR. ROBT. HERRICKE.

IV. *A Charroll presented to Dr.* Williams, *Bp. of Lincolne, as a Newyears Guift.*[3]

HYE hence, pale Care, noe more remember
 Past sorrowes with the fled December,
But let each plesant cheeke appeare
Smooth as the childhood of the yeare,
  And sing a carroll here.

---

[2] = use to want.   [3] From Ashmole MS. 36, 298. See Memorial-Introduction and also poem to this Bishop, Vol. I. p. 88.

'Twas braue, 'twas braue could we comand the hand
Of Youths swift watch to stand
As you haue done your day;
Then should we not decay,
But all we wither, & our light
Is spilt in euerlasting night,
When as your sight
Shewes like the heavens aboue ye moone
Like an eternall noone,
That sees no setting sunn.

Keepe vp those flames, & though you shroud
Awhile your forehead in a cloude,
Doe it like the sun to write
I'th ayre, a greater text of light;
Welcome to all our vowes,
And since you pay
To vs the day
Soe longe desir'd,
See we haue fyr'd
Our holy spicknard, and ther's none
But brings his stick of cynamon,
His eager eye, or smoother smyle;
And layes it gently on the pyle,
Which thus enkindled, we invoke
Your name amidst the sacred smoke.

Chorus. Come then, greate Lord,
      And see our Alter burne
      With love of your returne,
And not a man here but consumes
His soule to glad you in perfumes.
                        Rob : Herrick.

V. *Song. His Mistris to him at his Farwell.*[4]
YOU may vow Ile not forgett
      To pay the debt,
Which to thy Memorie stands as due
      As faith can seale It you :
Take then tribute of my teares,
      So long as I haue feares
      To prompt mee, I shall euer
Languiſh and looke, but thy returne see neuer :
      Oh then to leſsen my diſpaire,
      Print thy lips Into the ayre,
      So by this
Meanes, I may kiſse thy kiſse,
      whenas some kinde
      winde
shall hither waft it ; and In leiw,
My lipps shall send a 1000 back to you.
                        Ro : Herrick.

[4] From Additional MS. Br. Mus. 11,811, fol. 37.

VI. *Vpon Parting.*[5]

GOE hence away, and in thy parting know
    'tis not my voice, but heauens that bidds thee
        goe;
Spring hence thy faith, nor thinke it ill desart
I finde in thee, that makes me thus to part.
But voice of fame, and voice of heauen haue thunderd
we both were lost, if both of us not sunderd:
fould now thine armes, and in thy last looke reare
one Sighe of loue, and coole it with a teare:
since part we must, let's kisse; that done, retire
with as cold frost, as erst we mett with fire;
with such white vowes as fate can nere difsever
but truth knitt fast; and so farewell for euer.
                          R: HERRICK.

VII. *Upon Master Fletchers Incomparable Playes*[6].

APOLLO sings, his harpe refounds: give roome,
    For now behold the golden Pompe is come,
Thy Pompe of playes, which thoufands come to fee,
With admiration both of them and thee.

---

[5] From Harleian MS. 6,917, fol. 82 back.

[6] From Beaumont and Fletcher's Works, 1647: and in Beaumont's poems, 1653. See Dyce, Vol. 1. p. xlvii. In the original all in italic: names of the Plays Roman except *Love lyes a Bleeding*, which is in italic.

O Volume worthy, leafe by leafe, and cover,
To be with juice of Cedar [7] wash't all over;
Here's words with lines, and lines with fcenes confent,
To raife an Act to full aftonifhment;
Here melting numbers, words of power to move
Young men to fwoone, and Maides to dye for love.
Love lyes a bleeding here, Evadne, there
Swells with brave rage, yet comely every where;
Here's a *mad lover*, there that high defigne
Of *King and no King*, (and the rare Plott thine.)
So that whene'ere wee circumvolve [8] our Eyes,
Such rich, fuch frefh, fuch fweet varietyes,
Ravifh our fpirits, that entranc't wee see
None writes lov's paffion in the world, like thee.

       ROBERT HERRICK.

VIII. *THE NEW CHARON,*

Upon the Death of Henry *Lord* Hastings.[9]

The Musical part being set by M. Henry Lawes.

The Speakers,

Charon and *Eucofmeia.*

Euc. CHARON, O Charon, draw thy Boat to th' Shore,
  And to thy many, take in one foul more.

---

[7] See Glossarial Index s. v.   [8] See Glossarial Index s. v.
[9] From "Lachrymæ Musarum. The Tears of the Muses: exprest in Elegies written by divers persons of Nobility and Worth.

GOLDEN APPLES. 111

Cha. Who calls? who calls?   *Euc.* One overwhelm'd
  with ruth;
 Have pity either on my tears or Youth,
 And take me in, who am in deep Distress;
 But firſt caſt off thy wonted Churliſhneſs.
Cha. I will be gentle as that Air which yeelds
 A breath of Balm along th' *Elizean* fields.
 Speak, what art thou?   *Euc.* One, once that
  had a lover,   [*than*
 Then which, thy felf ne'er wafted fweeter over.
 He was——   *Cha.* Say what.   *Eu.* Ay me, my
  woes are deep.
Cha. Prethee relate, while I give ear and weep.
Euc. He was an *Hastings;* and that one Name has
 In it all good, that is, and ever was.
 He was my Life, my Love, my Joy; but di'd
 Some hours before I shou'd have been his Bride.
Chorus. *Thus, thus the gods celeſtial still decree,*
 For Humane Joy, Contingent Misery.
Euc. The *hallowed Tapers* all prepar̀ed were,
 And *Hymen* call'd to bleſs the Rites.   *Cha.* Stop
  there.

upon the death of the most hopefull Henry, Lord Hastings," &c. Collected and set forth by R[ichard] B[rome]. Lond. 1649, 8vo. pp. 38-9. See Memorial-Introduction on this in (probable) relation to his " Charon and Nightingale." As being printed (not MS.) the Roman and Italic intermixture of types has not been reproduced.

Euc. Great are my woes.   *Cha.* And great muſt that
    Grief be,
  That makes grim *Charon* thus to pity thee.
  But now come in.   *Euc.* More let me yet relate.
Cha. I cannot ſtay; more ſouls for waftage wait,
  And I muſt hence.   *Euc.* Yet let me thus much
    know,
  Departing hence, where Good and Bad ſouls go.
Cha. Thoſe ſouls which ne'er were drencht in plea-
    ſures ſtream,
  The Fields of *Pluto* are reſerv'd for them;
  Where, dreſt with garlands, there they walk
    the ground,
  Whose bleſsèd Youth with endleſs flow'rs is
    crown'd.
  But ſuch as have been drown'd in this wilde ſea,
  For thoſe is kept the Gulf of Hecatè;
  Where, with their own contagion they are fed;
  And there do puniſh, and are puniſhèd.
  This known, the reſt of thy ſad ſtory tell,
  When on the Flood that nine times circles Hell.
Chorus. *We ſail along, to viſit mortals never;*
  But there to live, where Love ſhall laſt for ever.
ROB. HERRICKE.

IX. *Epitaph on the Tomb of Sir* Edward Giles *& his wife in the South Aisle of Dean Prior Church, Devon.*[10]

NO truſt to Metalſ nor to Marbleſ, when
    Theſe have their Fate, and wear away aſ Men;
Timeſ, Titleſ, Trophieſ, may be loſt and Spent;
But Vertue Rearſ the eternal Monument.   [Pay?
What more than theſe can Tombſ or Tomb-ſtoneſ
But here'ſ the Sun-ſet of a Tediouſ day:
Theſe Two aſleep are: I'll but be Vndreſt
And ſo to Bed: Pray wiſh uſ all Good Reſt.

[10] See Memorial-Introduction on this hitherto inedited Epitaph.

NOTE.

It will be observed that the 'Noble Numbers' is dated 1647, which was doubtless 1647-8; and from the close of the 'Hesperides' it would seem Herrick intended 'Noble Numbers' to be prefixed, not affixed, thereto. See Memorial-Introduction for more on this. G.

HIS
NOBLE NUMBERS:
OR,
HIS PIOUS PIECES,

Wherein (amongſt other things)
He ſings the Birth of his CHRIST:
and ſighes for his *Saviours* ſuffe-
ring on the *Croſſe*.

HESIOD.

Ἴδμεν ψεύδεα πολλὰ λέγειν ἐτύμοισιν ὁμοῖα.
Ἴδμεν δ' εὖτ' ἐθέλωμεν, ἀληθέα μυθήσασθαι.

LONDON.
Printed for *John Williams*, and *Francis Eglesfield*.
1647.

HIS NOBLE NUMBERS:
OR,
HIS PIOUS PIECES.

His Confession.

LOOK how our foule Dayes do exceed
  our faire ;
And as our bad, more then our good
  Works are,   [than
Ev'n so those Lines, pen'd by my wanton Wit,
Treble the number of these good I've writ.
Things precious are least num'rous : Men are prone
To do ten Bad, for one Good Action.

His Prayer for Absolution.

FOR Those my unbaptizèd Rhimes,
  Writ in my wild unhallowéd Times ;[1]

---

[1] See Memorial-Introduction ; but 'unhallowed' here is simply = lay as opposed to clerical.

For every sentence, clause, and word,
That's not inlaid with Thee, (my Lord)
Forgive me, God, and blot each Line
Out of my Book, that is not Thine.
But if, 'mongst all, Thou find'st here one
Worthy thy Benediction;
That One of all the rest, shall be
The Glory of my Work, and Me.

To finde God.

WEIGH me the Fire; or canst thou find
    A way to measure out the Wind;
Distinguish all those Floods that are
Mixt in the watrie Theater;
And tast thou them as saltlesse there,
As in their Channell first they were.
Tell me the People that do keep
Within the Kingdomes of the Deep;
Or fetch me back that Cloud againe,
Beshiver'd[2] into seeds of Raine;
Tell me the motes, dust, sands, and speares[3]
Of Corn, when Summer shakes his eares;

---

[2] = all or wholly shivered.   [3] = spires or heads.

Shew me that world of Starres, and whence
They noiselesse spill their Influence :
This if thou canst ; then shew me Him
That rides the glorious *Cherubim*.[4]

What God is.

GOD is above the sphere of our esteem,
   And is the best known, not defining Him.

Upon God.

GOD is not onely said to be
   An *Ens*, but *Supraentitie*.[5]

Mercy and Love.

GOD hath two wings, which He doth ever move,
   The one is Mercy, and the next is Love :
Under the first the Sinners ever trust ;
And with the last he still directs the Just.

Gods Anger without Affection.

GOD when He's angry here with any one,
   His wrath is free from perturbation ;
And when we think His looks are sowre and grim,
The alteration is in us, not Him.

---

[4] Psalm lxviii. 4, 33.   [5] = above Being.

God not to be comprehended.

'TIS hard to finde God, but to comprehend
  Him, as He is, is labour without end.

Gods part.

PRAYERS and Praises are those spotlesse two
  Lambs, by the Law, which God requires as due.[6]

Affliction.

GOD n'ere afflicts us more then our desert,   [than
  Though He may seem to over-act His part:
Somtimes He strikes us more then flesh can beare;
But yet still lesse then Grace can suffer here.

Three fatall Sisters.

THREE fatall Sisters wait upon each sin;
  First, Fear and Shame without, then Guilt within.

Silence.

SUFFER thy legs, but not thy tongue to walk:
  God, the most Wise, is sparing of His talk.

---

[6] The cleansing sacrifice.   Cf. Numbers xxviii. 3 and 9, with Leviticus xiv. 10.

Mirth.

TRUE mirth resides not in the smiling skin :
   The sweetest solace is to act no sin.

Loading and unloading.

GOD loads, and unloads, (thus His work begins)
   To load with blessings, and unload from sins.

Gods Mercy.

GODS boundlesse mercy is (to sinfull man)
    Like to the ever-wealthy Ocean :
Which though it sends forth thousand streams, 'tis
      ne're
Known, or els seen to be the emptier;
And though it takes all in, 'tis yet no more
Full, and fild-full,[7] then when full-fild before.   [*than*

Prayers must have Poise.

GOD He rejects all Prayers that are sleight,
   And want their Poise : words ought to have
    their weight.

---

[7] See Glossarial Index s. v.

To God: an Anthem, sung in the Chappell at White-Hall, before the King.

Verse. MY God, I'm wounded by my sin,
 And sore without, and sick within :
Ver. Chor. I come to Thee, in hope to find
 Salve for my body, and my mind.
Verse. In *Gilead* though no Balme be found,
 To ease this smart, or cure this wound ;
Ver. Chor. Yet, Lord, I know there is with Thee
 All saving health, and help for me.
Verse. Then reach Thou forth that hand of
 Thine,
 That powres in oyle, as well as wine.
Ver. Chor. And let it work, for I'le endure
 The utmost smart, so Thou wilt cure.

Upon God.

GOD is all fore-part ; for, we never see
 Any part backward in the Deitie.

Calling, and correcting.

GOD is not onely mercifull, to call,
 Men to repent, but when He strikes withall.

No Escaping the scourging.

GOD scourgeth some severely, some He spares ;
 But all in smart have lesse, or greater shares.

The Rod.

GODS Rod doth watch while men do sleep, & then
The Rod doth sleep, while vigilant are men.

God has a twofold part.

GOD when for sin He makes His Children smart,
   His own He acts not, but anothers part:
But when by stripes He saves them, then 'tis known,
He comes to play the part that is His own.

God is One.

GOD, as He is most Holy knowne;
   So He is said to be most One.

Persecutions profitable.

AFFLICTIONS they most profitable are
   To the beholder, and the sufferer:
Bettering them both, but by a double straine,
The first by patience, and the last by paine.

To God.

DO with me, God! as Thou didst deal with *Iohn*,
   (Who writ that heavenly *Revelation*);

Let me (like him) first cracks of thunder heare;
Then let the Harps inchantments strike mine eare;
Here give me thornes; there, in thy Kingdome, set
Upon my head the golden coronet;
There give me day; but here my dreadfull night:
My sackcloth here; but there my *Stole* of white.

Whips.

GOD has His whips here to a twofold end,
  The bad to punish, and the good t'amend.

Gods Providence.

IF all transgressions here should have their pay,
  What need there then be of a reckning day?
If God should punish no sin, here, of men,
His Providence who would not question then?

Temptation.

THOSE Saints, which God loves best,
  The Devill tempts not least.

His Ejaculation to God.

MY God! looke on me with Thine eye
  Of pittie, not of scrutinie;
For if Thou dost, Thou then shalt see
Nothing but loathsome sores in mee.

O then! for mercies sake, behold
These my irruptions[8] manifold;
And heale me with Thy looke, or touch:
But if Thou wilt not deigne so much,
Because I'm odious in Thy sight,
Speak but the word, and cure me quite.

Gods gifts not soone granted.

GOD heares us when we pray, but yet defers
   His gifts, to exercise Petitioners:
And though awhile He makes Requesters stay,
With Princely hand He'l recompence delay.

Persecutions purifie.

GOD strikes His Church, but 'tis to this intent,
   To make, not marre her, by this punishment:
So where He gives the bitter Pills, be sure,
'Tis not to poyson, but to make thee pure.

Pardon.

GOD pardons those, who do through frailty sin;
   But never those that persevere therein.

---

[8]. = eruptions.

An Ode of the Birth of our Saviour.

1. IN Numbers, and but these few,
    I sing Thy Birth, Oh JESU !
   Thou prettie Babie, borne here,
   With sup'rabundant scorn here :
   Who for Thy Princely Port here,
        Hadst for Thy place
        Of Birth, a base
   Out-stable for thy Court here.

2. Instead of neat Inclosures
   Of inter-woven Osiers ;[9]
   Instead of fragrant Posies
   Of Daffadills, and Roses ;
   Thy cradle, Kingly Stranger,
        As Gospell tells,
        Was nothing els,
   But, here, a homely manger.

3. But we with Silks, (not Cruells,[10])
   With sundry precious Jewells,
   And Lilly-work will dresse Thee ;
   And as we dispossesse Thee

---

[9] = cradles.   [10] = worsted used for fancy needle-work.

Of clouts, wee'l make a chamber,
        Sweet Babe, for Thee,
    Of Ivorie,
And plaister'd round with Amber.

4. The Jewes they did disdaine Thee,
But we will entertaine Thee
With Glories to await here
Upon Thy Princely State here,
And more for love, then pittie.   [*than*
      From yeere to yeere
      Wee'l make Thee, here,
A Free-born of our Citie.

Lip-labour.

IN the old Scripture I have often read,
    The calfe without meale n'ere was offerèd;
To figure to us, nothing more then this,   [*than*
Without the heart, lip-labour nothing is.

The Heart.

IN Prayer the Lips ne're act the winning part,
    Without the sweet concurrence of the Heart.

Eare-rings.

WHY wore th' Egyptians Jewells in the Eare?
    But for to teach us, all the grace is there,
When we obey, by acting what we heare.

Sin seen.

WHEN once the sin has fully acted been,
    Then is the horror of the trespasse seen.

Upon Time.

TIME was upon
    The wing, to flie away;
    And I cal'd on
Him but awhile to stay;
    But he'd be gone,
For ought that I could say.

He held out then,
A Writing, as he went;
    And askt me, when
False man would be content
    To pay agen,
What God and Nature lent.

An houre-glasse,
In which were sands but few,
As he did passe,
He shew'd and told me too,
Mine end near was,
And so away he flew.

His Petition.

IF warre, or want shall make me grow so poore,
   As for to beg my bread from doore to doore;
Lord! let me never act that beggars part,
Who hath Thee in his mouth, not in his heart.[1]
He who asks almes in that so sacred Name,
Without due reverence, playes the cheaters game.

To God.

THOU hast promis'd, Lord, to be
   With me in my miserie;
Suffer me to be so bold,
As to speak, Lord, say and hold.[2]

---

[1] Cf. Ezekiel xxxiii. 31.
[2] Apparently a known and proverbial phrase = say and hold to it, i. e. perform thy promise.

His Letanie, to the Holy Spirit.

1. IN the houre of my distresse,
    When temptations me oppresse,
    And when I my sins confesse,
        Sweet Spirit comfort me!

2. When I lie within my bed,
    Sick in heart and sick in head,
    And with doubts discomforted,
        Sweet Spirit comfort me!

3. When the house doth sigh and weep,
    And the world is drown'd in sleep,
    Yet mine eyes the watch do keep;
        Sweet Spirit comfort me!

4. When the artlesse[3] Doctor sees
    No one hope, but of his Fees,
    And his skill runs on the lees;
        Sweet Spirit comfort me!

5. When his Potion and his Pill,
    Has, or none, or little skill,
    Meet for nothing, but to kill;
        Sweet Spirit comfort me!

---

[3] = unskilful. See Memorial-Introduction on this (II. Critical).

6. When the passing-bell doth tole,
   And the Furies in a shole
   Come to fright a parting soule ;
       Sweet Spirit comfort me !

7. When the tapers now burne blew,
   And the comforters are few,
   And that number more then true ;[4]   [*than*
       Sweet Spirit comfort me !

8. When the Priest his last hath praid,
   And I nod to what is said,
   'Cause my speech is now decaid ;
       Sweet Spirit comfort me !

9. When (God knowes) I'm tost about,
   Either with despaire, or doubt ;
   Yet before the glasse be out,
       Sweet Spirit comfort me !

10. When the Tempter me pursu'th
    With the sins of all my youth,
    And halfe damns me with untruth ;
        Sweet Spirit comfort me !

---

[4] = and when the few that gather around me are not all true friends or comforters.

11. When the flames and hellish cries
    Fright mine eares, and fright mine eyes,
    And all terrors me surprize;
        Sweet Spirit comfort me!

12. When the Judgment is reveal'd,
    And that open'd which was seal'd,
    When to Thee I have appeal'd;
        Sweet Spirit comfort me!

Thanksgiving.

THANKSGIVING for a former, doth invite
    God to bestow a second benefit.

Cock-crow.

BELL-MAN of Night,[5] if I about shall go
    For to denie my Master, do thou crow.
Thou stop'st S. *Peter* in the midst of sin;
Stay me, by crowing, ere I do begin;
Better it is, premonish'd, for to shun
A sin, then fall to weeping when 'tis done.   [than

---

[5] The cock. So Spenser:
    ——— "Bell-man of the night,
   The bird that warnèd Peter of his fall." Fairy Queen.

All Things run well for the Righteous.

ADVERSE and prosperous Fortunes both work on
   Here, for the righteous mans salvation :
Be he oppos'd, or be he not withstood,
All serve to th' Augmentation of his good.

Paine ends in Pleasure.

AFFLICTIONS bring us joy in times to come,
   When sins, by stripes, to us grow wearisome.

To God.

I'LE come, I'le creep, (though Thou dost threat,)
   Humbly unto Thy Mercy-seat :
When I am there, this then I'le do,
Give Thee a Dart, and Dagger too ;
Next, when I have my faults confest,
Naked I'le shew a sighing brest ;
Which if that can't Thy pittie wooe,
Then let Thy Justice do the rest,
      And strike it through.

A Thanksgiving to God, for His House.

LORD, Thou hast given me a cell
      Wherein to dwell ;

A little house, whose humble Roof
        Is weather-proof;
Under the sparres of which I lie
        Both soft, and drie;
Where Thou my chamber for to ward
        Hast set a Guard
Of harmlesse thoughts, to watch and keep
        Me, while I sleep.
Low is my porch, as is my Fate,
        Both void of state;
And yet the threshold of my doore
        Is worn by th' poore,
Who thither come, and freely get
        Good words, or meat:
Likeas my Parlour, so my Hall
        And Kitchin's small:
A little Butterie, and therein
        A little Byn,
Which keeps my little loafe of Bread
        Unchipt, unflead:[6]
Some brittle sticks of Thorne or Briar
        Make me a fire,
Close by whose living coale I sit,
        And glow like it.

---

[6] Probably = good, undamaged by mould, &c. Halliwell has 'fled' as a Shropshire word.

Lord, I confesse too, when I dine,
       The Pulse is Thine,
And all those other Bits, that bee
       There plac'd by Thee;
The Worts,[7] the Purslain,[8] and the Messe
       Of water-cresse,
Which of Thy kindnesse Thou hast sent;
       And my content
Makes those, and my belovèd Beet,
       To be more sweet.
'Tis Thou that crown'st my glittering Hearth
       With guiltlesse mirth;
And giv'st me Wassaile Bowles to drink,
       Spic'd to the brink.
Lord, 'tis Thy plenty-dropping hand,
       That soiles[9] my land;
And giv'st me, for my Bushell sowne,
       Twice ten for one:
Thou mak'st my teeming Hen to lay
       Her egg each day:
Besides my healthfull Ewes to beare
       Me twins each yeare:
The while the conduits of my Kine
       Run Creame, (for Wine.)

---

[7] = cabbage.   [8] A kind of sallad. See Glossarial Index s. v.
[9] = manures.

All these, and better Thou dost send
  Me, to this end,
That I should render, for my part,
  A thankfull heart;
Which, fir'd with incense, I resigne,
  As wholly Thine;
But the acceptance, that must be,
  My Christ, by Thee.

To God.

MAKE, make me Thine, my gracious God,
 Or with Thy staffe, or with Thy rod;
And be the blow too what it will,
Lord, I will kisse it, though it kill:
Beat me, bruise me, rack me, rend me,
Yet, in torments, I'le commend Thee:
Examine me with fire, and prove me
To the full, yet I will love Thee:
Nor shalt Thou give so deep a wound,
But I as patient will be found.

Another, to God.

LORD, do not beat me,
 Since I do sob and crie,
And swowne away to die,

Ere Thou dost threat me.
Lord, do not scourge me,
If I by lies and oaths
Have soil'd my selfe, or cloaths,
But rather purge me.

None truly happy here.

HAPPY'S that man, to whom God gives
  A stock of Goods, whereby he lives
Neer to the wishes of his heart:
No man is blest through ev'ry part.

To his ever-loving God.

CAN I not come to Thee, my God, for these
  So very-many-meeting hindrances,
That slack my pace; but yet not make me stay?
Who slowly goes, rids[1] (in the end) his way.
Cleere Thou my paths, or shorten Thou my miles,
Remove the barrs, or lift me o're the stiles:
Since rough the way is, help me when I call,
And take me up; or els prevent the fall.
I kenn[2] my home; and it affords some ease,
To see far off the smoaking Villages.

---

[1] = gets rid or clear of his way, i. e. finishes his journey.
[2] = know.

Fain would I rest ; yet covet not to die,
For feare of future-biting penurie :
No, no, (my God) Thou know'st my wishes be
To leave this life, not loving it, but Thee.

Another.

THOU bidst me come ; I cannot come ; for why,
   Thou dwel'st aloft, and I want wings to flie.
To mount my Soule, she must have pineons given ;
For, 'tis no easie way from Earth to Heaven.

To Death.

THOU bidst me come away,
   And I'le no longer stay,
Then for to shed some teares   [than
For faults of former yeares ;
And to repent some crimes,
Done in the present times :
And next, to take a bit
Of Bread, and Wine with it :
To d'on my robes of love,
Fit for the place above ;
To gird my loynes about
With charity throughout ;

And so to travaile hence
With feet of innocence:
These done, I'le onely crie
God mercy; and so die.

Neutrality loathsome.

GOD will have all, or none; serve Him, or fall
   Down before *Baal, Bel,* or *Belial:*
Either be hot, or cold: God doth despise,
Abhorre, and spew out all Neutralities.[3]

Welcome what comes.

WHATEVER comes, let's be content withall:
   Among God's Blessings, there is no one small.

To his angrie God.

THROUGH all the night
   Thou dost me fright,
And hold'st mine eyes from sleeping;
   And day, by day,
   My Cup can say,
My wine is mixt with weeping.

Thou dost my bread
With ashes knead,
Each evening and each morrow:

---

[3] Revelation, c. iii. v. 16.

Mine eye and eare
Do see, and heare
The coming in of sorrow.

Thy scourge of steele,
(Ay me!) I feele,
Upon me beating ever:
While my sick heart
With dismall smart
Is disacquainted never.

Long, long, I'm sure,
This can't endure;
But in short time 'twill please Thee,
My gentle God,
To burn the rod,
Or strike so as to ease me.

Patience, or Comforts in Crosses.

ABUNDANT plagues I late have had,
   Yet none of these have made me sad
For why, my Saviour, with the sense
Of suffring gives me patience.

Eternitie.

1. O YEARES! and Age! Farewell:
   Behold I go,

      Where I do know
Infinitie to dwell.

2. And these mine eyes shall see
      All times, how they
      Are lost i' th' Sea
Of vast Eternitie.

3. Where never Moone shall sway
      The Starres ; but she,
      And Night, shall be
Drown'd in one endlesse Day.

To his Saviour, a Child; a Present, by a child.

GO prettie child, and beare this Flower
    Unto thy little Saviour ;
And tell Him, by that Bud now blown,
He is the *Rose of Sharon* known :
When thou hast said so, stick it there
Upon His Bibb, or Stomacher :
And tell Him, (for good handsell [4] too)
That thou hast brought a Whistle new,
Made of a clean strait oaten reed,
To charme His cries, (at time of need :)

[4] See Glossarial Index s. v.

Tell Him, for Corall, thou hast none ;
But if thou hadst, He sho'd have one ;
But poore thou art, and knowne to be
Even as monilesse, as He.
Lastly, if thou canst win a kisse
From those mellifluous lips of His ;
Then never take a second on,
To spoile the first impression.

The New-yeeres Gift.

LET others looke for Pearle and Gold,
    Tissues, or Tabbies [5] manifold :
One onely lock of that sweet Hay
Whereon the blessed Babie lay,
Or one poore Swadling-clout, shall be
The richest New-yeeres Gift to me.

To God.

IF any thing delight me for to print
    My Book, 'tis this ; that, *Thou, my God, art in't.*

God, and the King.

HOW am I bound to Two ! God, who doth give
    The mind ; the King, the meanes whereby I live.

---

[5] = kind of thick-threaded silk watered by presses. See Glossarial Index s. v : cloth, called 'tabby : ' and we still have 'tabinet : ' qu. —as resembling the smooth coat of a cat 'Tabby.'

Gods mirth, Mans mourning.

WHERE God is merry, there write down thy
    fears :
What He with laughter speaks, heare thou with tears.

Honours are hindrances.

GIVE me Honours ! what are these,
    But the pleasing hindrances ?
Stiles, and stops, and stayes, that come
In the way 'twixt me, and home :
Cleer the walk, and then shall I
To my heaven lesse run, then flie.   [*than*

The Parasceve, or Preparation.

TO a Love-Feast we both invited are :
    The figur'd Damask, or pure Diaper,[6]
Over the golden Altar now is spread,
With Bread, and Wine, and Vessells furnishèd ;
The *sacred Towell*, and the *holy Eure*[7]
Are ready by, to make the Guests all pure :
Let's go (my *Alma*)[8] yet, e're we receive,
Fit, fit it is, we have our *Parasceve.*[9]
Who to that *sweet Bread* unprepar'd doth come,
Better he starv'd, then but to tast one crumme.   [*than*

[6] = figured linen. See Glossarial Index s. v.
[7] = flagon.   [8] = pure one, virgin.   [9] = preparation.

To God.

GOD gives not onely corne, for need,
  But likewise sup'rabundant seed ;
Bread for our service, bread for shew ;
Meat for our meales, and fragments too :
He gives not poorly, taking some
Between the finger, and the thumb ;
But, for our glut, and for our store,
Fine flowre prest down, and running o're.

A will to be working.

ALTHOUGH we cannot turne the fervent fit
  Of sin, we must strive 'gainst the streame of it :
And howsoe're we have the conquest mist ;
'Tis for our glory, that we did resist.

Christs part.

CHRIST, He requires still, wheresoere He comes,
  To feed, or lodge, to have the best of Roomes :
Give Him the choice ; grant Him the nobler part
Of all the House : the best of all's the Heart.

Riches and Poverty.

GOD co'd have made all rich, or all men poore ;
  But why He did not, let me tell wherefore :

Had all been rich, where then had Patience been?
Had all been poore, who had His Bounty seen?

Sobriety in Search.

TO seek of God [1] more then we well can find,   [*than*
    Argues a strong distemper of the mind.

Almes.

GIVE, if thou canst, an Almes; if not, afford,
    Instead of that, a sweet and gentle word:
God crowns our goodnesse, wheresoere He sees,
On our part, wanting all abilities.

To his Conscience.

CAN I not sin, but thou wilt be
    My private *Protonotarie?* [2]
Can I not wooe thee to passe by
    A short and sweet iniquity?
I'le cast a mist and cloud, upon
    My delicate transgression,
So utter dark, as that no eye
    Shall see the hug'd [3] impietie:

---

[1] i.e. to seek into the nature and acts of God.
[2] =prothonotary, or chief recording scribe, as in the courts of law.
[3] =hugged. See similarly Glossarial Index under 'rag'd' for 'ragged.'

Gifts blind the wise, and bribes do please,
And winde all other witnesses:
And wilt not thou, with gold, be ti'd
To lay thy pen and ink aside?
That in the mirk[4] and tonguelesse night,
Wanton I may, and thou not write?
It will not be: And, therefore, now,
For times to come, I'le make this Vow,
From aberrations to live free;
So I'le not feare the Judge, or thee.

To his Saviour.

LORD, I confesse, that Thou alone art able
   To purifie this my *Augean* stable:
Be the Seas water, and the Land all Sope,
Yet if Thy Bloud not wash me, there's no hope.

To God.

GOD is all-sufferance here; here He doth show
   No Arrow nockt,[5] onely a stringlesse Bow:
His Arrowes flie, and all his stones are hurl'd
Against the wicked, in another world.

His Dreame.

I DREAMT, last night, Thou didst transfuse
   Oyle from Thy Jarre, into my creuze;

---

[4] = dark. [5] = The nock or noch of the arrow set in the bow-string

And powring still, Thy wealthy store,
The vessell full, did then run ore :
Me thought, I did Thy bounty chide,
To see the waste; but 'twas repli'd
By Thee, Deare God, God gives man seed
Oft-times for wast, as for his need.
Then I co'd say, that house is bare,
That has not bread, and some to spare.[6]

Gods Bounty.

GODS Bounty, that ebbs lesse and lesse,
   As men do wane in thankfulnesse.

To his sweet Saviour.

NIGHT hath no wings, to him that cannot sleep;
   And Time seems then, not for to flie, but creep;
Slowly her chariot drives, as if that she
Had broke her wheele, or crackt her axeltree.
Just so it is with me, who list'ning, pray
The winds, to blow the tedious night away;
That I might see the cheerfull peeping day.
Sick is my heart ! O Saviour ! do Thou please
To make my bed soft in my sicknesses:

---

[6] A reference to "Exilis domus est, ubi non et multa supersunt, &c. Horace, Ep. I. vi. l. 45.

Lighten my candle, so that I beneath
Sleep not for ever in the vaults of death :
Let me Thy voice betimes i' th' morning heare ;
Call, and I'le come ; say Thou, the when, and where
Draw me but first, and after Thee I'le run,
And make no one stop, till my race be done.

His Creed.

I DO believe, that die I must,
    And be return'd from out my dust :
I do believe, that when I rise,
Christ I shall see, with these same eyes :
I do believe, that I must come,
With others, to the dreadfull Doome : [7]
I do believe, the bad must goe
From thence, to everlasting woe :
I do believe, the good, and I,
Shall live with Him eternally :
I do believe, I shall inherit
Heaven, by Christs mercies, not my merit :
I do believe, the One in Three,
And Three in perfect Unitie :
Lastly, that JESUS is a Deed
Of Gift from God : *And heres my Creed.*

[7] See Glossarial Index s. v.

Temptations.

TEMPTATIONS hurt not, though they have
    accesse:
Satan o'ercomes none, but by willingnesse.

The Lamp.

WHEN a man's Faith is frozen up, as dead;
    Then is the Lamp and oyle extinguishèd.

Sorrowes.

SORROWES our portion are: Ere hence we goe,
    Crosses we must have; or, hereafter woe.

Penitencie.

A MANS transgression God do's then remit,
    When man he makes a Penitent for it.

The Dirge of Jephthahs *Daughter: sung
    by the Virgins.*

1. O THOU, the wonder of all dayes!
    O Paragon,[8] and Pearle of praise!
  O Virgin-martyr, ever blest
        Above the rest

---

[8] The highest or most precious, chief among virgins. See quotation from Gough in Nares s. v. The origin of the phrase may be doubtful, but probably it is from the eye being so bright and precious a part of the body.

Of all the Maiden-Traine ! We come,
And bring fresh strewings to thy Tombe.

2. Thus, thus, and thus we compasse round
Thy harmlesse and unhaunted Ground;
And as we sing thy Dirge, we will
      The Daffadill,
And other flowers, lay upon
(The Altar of our love) thy Stone.

3. Thou wonder of all Maids, li'st here,
Of Daughters all, the Deerest Deere;
The eye of Virgins;[9] nay, the Queen,
      Of this smooth Green,
And all sweet Meades; from whence we get
The Primrose, and the Violet.

4. Too soon, too deere did *Jephthah* buy,
By thy sad losse, our liberty :
His was the Bond and Cov'nant, yet
      Thou paid'st the debt :
Lamented Maid ! he won the day,
But for the conquest thou didst pay.

[9] See Glossarial Index s. v.

5. Thy Father brought with him along
   The Olive branch, and Victors Song:
   He slew the Ammonites,[1] we know,
             But to thy woe;
   And in the purchase of our Peace,
   The Cure was worse then the Disease.   [*than*

6. For which obedient zeale of thine,
   We offer here, before thy Shrine,
   Our sighs for Storax, teares for Wine;
             And to make fine,
   And fresh thy Herse-cloth,[2] we will, here,
   Foure times bestrew thee ev'ry yeere.

7. Receive, for this thy praise, our teares:
   Receive this offering of our Haires:[3]
   Receive these Christall Vialls fil'd
             With teares, distil'd
   From teeming eyes; to these we bring,
   Each Maid, her silver Filleting,

---

[1] Cf. Judges xi. 1—33.
[2] Here metaphorical for the turf or tomb covering her.
[3] Referring to the Eastern custom of shaving or cutting the hair in token of grief. Cf. Job. i. 30: Jer. vii. 29.

8. To guild thy Tombe ; besides, these Caules,[4]
   These Laces, Ribbands, and these Faules,
   These Veiles, wherewith we use to hide
                   The Bashfull Bride,
   When we conduct her to her Groome :
   And, all we lay upon thy Tombe.

9. No more, no more, since thou art dead,
   Shall we ere bring coy Brides to bed ;
   No more, at yeerly Festivalls
                   We Cowslip balls,
   Or chaines of Columbines [5] shall make,
   For this, or that occasions sake.

10. No, no ; our Maiden-pleasures be
    Wrapt in the winding-sheet, with thee :
    'Tis we are dead, though not i' th' grave :
                    Or, if we have
    One seed of life left, 'tis to keep
    A Lent for thee, to fast and weep.

11. Sleep in thy peace, thy bed of Spice ;
    And make this place all Paradise :
    May Sweets grow here ! & smoke from hence,
                    Fat Frankincense :

---

[4] = curls or head-dresses.   [5] Flowers so named.

Let Balme and Cassia, send their scent
From out thy Maiden-Monument.

12. May no Wolfe howle, or Screech-Owle stir
    A wing about thy Sepulcher!
    No boysterous winds, or stormes, come hither,
        To starve, or wither
    Thy soft sweet Earth! but (like a spring)
    Love keep it ever flourishing.

13. May all shie Maids, at wonted hours,
    Come forth, to strew thy Tombe with flow'rs:
    May Virgins, when they come to mourn,
        Male-Incense burn[6]
    Upon thine Altar! then return,
    And leave thee sleeping in thy Urn.

To God, on his sicknesse.

WHAT though my Harp, and Violl be
  Both hung upon the Willow-tree?
What though my bed be now my grave,
And for my house I darknesse have?
What though my healthfull dayes are fled,
And I lie numbred with the dead?
Yet I have hope, by Thy great power,
To spring; though now a wither'd flower.

[6] See Glossarial Index s. v.

Sins loath'd, and yet lov'd.

SHAME *checks our first attempts;* but then 'tis prov'd,
Sins first dislik'd, are after that belov'd.[7]

Sin.

SIN leads the way, but as it goes, it feels
    The following plague still treading on his heels.

Upon God.

GOD when He takes my goods and chattels hence
    Gives me a portion, giving patience :
What is in God is God ; if so it be,
He patience gives ; He gives himselfe to me.

Faith.

WHAT here we hope for, we shall once[8] inherit :
    By Faith we all walk here, not by the Spirit.

Humility.

HUMBLE we must be, if to Heaven we go :
    High is the roof there ; but the gate is low :
When e're thou speak'st, look with a lowly eye :
Grace is increasèd by humility.

---

[7] See Memorial-Introduction for a parallel later (in Pope).
[8] = at some future time and continuously, once and for aye.

Teares.

OUR present Teares here (not our present laughter)
Are but the handsells of our joyes[9] hereafter.

Sin and Strife.

AFTER true sorrow for our sinnes, our strife
Must last with Satan, to the end of life.

An Ode, or Psalme, to God.

DEER God,
    If thy smart Rod
Here did not make me sorrie,
    I sho'd not be
    With Thine, or Thee,
In Thy eternall Glorie.

    But since
    Thou didst convince
My sinnes, by gently striking;
    Add still to those
    First stripes, new blowes;
According to Thy liking.

---

[9] Cf. Herbert: (Vol. i. p. 65, l. 13, F. W. Library edn.) "Thou art Joye's handsell."

Feare me,[1]
Or scourging teare me;
That thus from vices driven,
I may from Hell
Flie up, to dwell
With Thee, and Thine in Heaven.

Graces for Children.

WHAT God gives, and what we take,
'Tis a gift for Christ His sake:
Be the meale of Beanes and Pease,
God be thank'd for those, and these:
Have we flesh, or have we fish,
All are Fragments from His dish.
He His Church save, and the King,
And our Peace here, like a Spring,
Make it ever flourishing.

God to be first serv'd.

HONOUR thy Parents; but good manners call
Thee to adore thy God, the first of all.

Another Grace for a Child.

HERE a little child I stand,
Heaving up my either hand;

[1] = make me afraid.

Cold as Paddocks[2] though they be,
Here I lift them up to Thee,
For a Benizon[3] to fall
On our meat, and on us all. *Amen.*

A Christmas Caroll, *sung to the King in the Presence at* White-Hall.[4]

Chor. WHAT sweeter musick can we bring,
    Then a Caroll, for to sing   [*than*
The Birth of this our heavenly King?
Awake the Voice! awake the String!
Heart, Eare, and Eye, and every thing
Awake! the while the active Finger
Runs division with the Singer.

From the Flourish they came to the Song.

1. Dark and dull night, flie hence away,
   And give the honour to this Day,
   That sees *December* turn'd to *May.*

2. If we may ask the reason, say;
   The why, and wherefore all things here
   Seem like the Spring-time of the yeere?

---

[2] = frogs.   [3] = benison, benediction.
[4] See Memorial-Introduction.

3. Why do's the chilling Winters morne
Smile, like a field beset with corne?
Or smell, like to a Meade new-shorne,
Thus, on the sudden? 4. Come and see
The cause, why things thus fragrant be:
'Tis He is borne, whose quickning Birth
Gives life and luster, publike mirth,
To Heaven, and the under-Earth.

Chor. We see Him come, and know him ours,
Who, with His Sun-shine, and His showers,
Turnes all the patient ground to flowers.

1. The Darling of the world is come,
And fit it is, we finde a roome
To welcome Him. 2. The nobler part
Of all the house here, is the heart,

Chor. Which we will give Him ; and bequeath
This Hollie, and this Ivie Wreath,
To do Him honour ; who's our King,
And Lord of all this Revelling.

The Musicall Part was composed by
M. Henry Lawes.

*The New-yeeres Gift, or Circumcisions Song,
sung to the King in the Presence at
White-Hall.*[5]

1. PREPARE for Songs ; He's come, He's come ;
And be it sin here to be dumb,
And not with Lutes to fill the roome.

2. Cast Holy Water all about,
And have a care no fire gos out,
But 'cense the porch and place, throughout.

3. The Altars all on fier be ;
The Storax fries ; and ye may see,
How heart and hand do all agree,
To make things sweet.   *Chor.* Yet all less sweet
then He.   [*than*

4. Bring Him along, most pious Priest,
And tell us then, whenas thou seest
His gently-gliding, Dove-like eyes,
And hear'st His whimp'ring, and His cries ;
How canst thou this Babe circumcise ?

[5] Ibid.

5. Ye must not be more pitifull then wise; [*than*
   For, now unlesse ye see Him bleed,
   Which makes the Bapti'me;[6] 'tis decreed,
The Birth is fruitlesse: *Chor.* Then the *work God
      speed.*

1. Touch gently, gently touch; and here
   Spring Tulips up through all the yeere;
   And from His sacred Bloud, here shed,
May Roses grow, to crown His own deare Head.

Chor. Back, back again; each thing is done
   With zeale alike, as 'twas begun;
   Now singing, homeward let us carrie
   The Babe unto His Mother *Marie;*
   And when we have the Child commended
To her warm bosome, then our Rites are ended.

Composed by M. Henry Lawes.

*Another New-yeeres Gift, or Song for
   the Circumcision.*

1. HENCE, hence prophane, and none appeare
   With any thing unhallowed, here:

---

[6] See Glossarial Index s. v.

No jot of Leven must be found
Conceal'd in this most holy Ground :[7]

2. What is corrupt, or sowr'd with sin,
Leave that without, then enter in ;

Chor. But let no Christmas mirth begin
Before ye purge, and circumcise
Your hearts, and hands, lips, eares, and eyes.

3. Then, like a perfum'd Altar, see
That all things sweet, and clean may be :
For, here's a Babe, that (like a *Bride*)
Will *blush to death*, if ought be spi'd
Ill-scenting, or unpurifi'd.

Chor. The room is cens'd :[8] help, help t'invoke
Heaven to come down, the while we choke
The Temple, with a cloud of smoke.

4. Come then, and gently touch the Birth
Of Him, Who's Lord of Heav'n and Earth ;

5. And softly handle Him : y'ad need,
Because the *prettie Babe* do's bleed.
Poore-pittied Child ! Who from Thy Stall

---

[7] Exodus xxxiv. 25.   [8] See Glossarial Index s. v.

Bring'st, in Thy Blood, a Balm, that shall
Be the best New-yeares Gift to all.

1. Let's blesse the Babe : And, as we sing
His praise ; so let us blesse the King :

Chor. Long may He live, till He hath told
His New-yeeres trebled to His old :
And, when that's done, to re-aspire
A new-borne *Phœnix* from His own chast fire.

Gods Pardon.

WHEN I shall sin, pardon my trespasse here ;
   For, once in hell, none knowes Remission there

Sin.

SIN once reacht up to Gods eternall Sphere,[9]
   And was committed, not remitted there.

Evill.

EVILL no Nature hath ; the losse of good
   Is that which gives to sin a livelihood.

---

[9] Referring to Satan's rebellion.

*The Star-Song: a Caroll to the King;
sung at White-Hall.*[1]

The Flourish of Musick: then followed the Song.

1. TELL us, thou cleere and heavenly Tongue,
     Where is the Babe but lately sprung?
   Lies He the Lillie-banks among?

2. Or say, if this new Birth of ours
   Sleeps, laid within some Ark of Flowers,
   Spangled with deaw-light; thou canst cleere
   All doubts, and manifest the where.

3. Declare to us, bright Star, if we shall seek
   Him in the Mornings blushing cheek,
   Or search the beds of Spices through,
   To find him out?

Star. No, this ye need not do;
   But only come, and see Him rest
   A Princely Babe in's Mothers Brest.

Chor. He's seen, He's seen, why then a Round,[2]
   Let's kisse the sweet and holy ground;
   And all rejoyce, that we have found
   A King, before conception crown'd.

---

[1] See Memorial-Introduction. [2] = a dance.

4. Come then, come then, and let us bring
   Unto our prettie *Twelfth-Tide King*,[3]
   Each one his severall offering;

Chor. And when night comes, wee'l give Him
             wassailing;
And that His treble Honours may be seen,
Wee'l chuse Him King, and make His Mother Queen.

To God.

WITH golden Censers, and with Incense, here,
Before Thy Virgin-Altar I appeare,
To pay Thee that I owe, since what I see
In, or without; all, all belongs to Thee:
Where shall I now begin to make, for one
Least loane of Thine, half Restitution?
Alas! I cannot pay a jot; therefore
I'le kisse the Tally,[4] and confesse the score.[5]
Ten thousand Talents lent me, Thou dost write:
'Tis true, my God; *but I can't pay one mite.*

To his deere God.

I'LE hope no more,
     For things that will not come:
And, if they do, they prove but cumbersome;

---

[3] The 'Holy Child' Jesus.
[4] = the notched stick for marking of debts.   [5] = debts.

Wealth brings much woe:
And, since it fortunes so;
'Tis better to be poore,
Than so t'abound,
As to be drown'd,
Or overwhelm'd with store.

Pale care, avant,
I'le learn to be content
With that small stock, Thy Bounty gave or lent.
What may conduce
To my most healthfull use,
Almighty God me grant;
But that, or this,
That hurtfull is,
Denie Thy suppliant.

To God, his good will.

GOLD I have none, but I present my need,
   O Thou, that crown'st the will, where wants
     the deed.
Where Rams are wanting, or large Bullocks thighs,
There a poor Lamb's a plenteous sacrifice.
Take then his Vowes, who, if he had it, would
Devote to Thee, both incense, myrrhe, and gold,
Upon an Altar rear'd by Him, and crown'd
Both with the *Rubie, Pearle,* and *Diamond.*

On Heaven.

PERMIT mine eyes to see
    Part, or the whole of Thee,
    O happy place!
    Where all have Grace,
    And Garlands shar'd,
    For their reward;
    Where each chast Soule
    In long white stole,
    And Palmes in hand,
    Do ravisht stand;
    So in a ring,
    The praises sing
    Of Three in One,
    That fill the Throne;
    While Harps, and Violls then
    To Voices, say, *Amen.*

The Summe, and the Satisfaction.

LAST night I drew up mine Account,
    And found my Debits to amount
To such a height, as for to tell
How I sho'd pay, 's impossible:
Well, this I'le do; my mighty score
Thy mercy-seat I'le lay before;

But therewithall I'le bring the Band,
Which, in full force, did daring[6] stand,
Till my Redeemer (on the Tree)
Made void for millions, as for me.
Then, if Thou bidst me pay, or go
Unto the prison, I'le say, no ;
Christ having paid, I nothing owe :
For, this is sure, the Debt is dead
By Law, the Bond once *cancellèd*.

Good men afflicted most.

GOD makes not good men wantons, but doth bring
Them to the field, and, there, to skirmishing ;
With trialls those, with terrors these He proves,
And hazards those most, whom the most He loves ;
For *Sceva*, darts ; for *Cocles*, dangers ; thus
He finds a fire for mighty *Mutius ;*
Death for stout *Cato ;* and besides all these,
A poyson too He has for *Socrates ;*
Torments for high *Attilius ;* and, with want,
Brings in *Fabricius* for a Combatant :[7]

---

[6] = frightening, causing fear—a hawking and bird-catching term.
[7] All the names herein are classical commonplaces, and need no annotation.

But, bastard-slips, and such as He dislikes,
He never brings them once to th' push of Pikes.[8]

Good Christians.

PLAY their offensive and defensive parts,
  Till they be hid o're with a wood of darts.

The Will the cause of Woe.

WHEN man is punisht, he is plaguèd still,
  Not for the fault of Nature, but of will.

To Heaven.

OPEN thy gates
  To him, who weeping waits,
  And might come in,
But that held back by sin.
  Let mercy be
So kind, to set me free,
  And I will strait
Come in, or force the gate.

The Recompence.

ALL I have lost, that co'd be rapt from me;
  And fare it well: yet *Herrick*, if so be

---

[8] Hebrews xii. 8 = danger or affliction.

Thy Deerest Saviour renders thee but one
Smile, that one smile's full restitution.

To God.

PARDON me God, (once more I Thee intreat)
    That I have plac'd Thee in so meane a seat,
Where round about Thou seest but all things vaine,
Uncircumcis'd, unseason'd, and prophane.
But as Heavens publike and immortall Eye
Looks on the filth, but is not soil'd thereby;
So Thou, my God, may'st on this impure, look,
But take no tincture from my sinfull Book:
Let but one beame of Glory on it shine,
And that will make me, and my Work divine.[9]

To God.

LORD, I am like to *Misletoe*,
    Which has no root, and cannot grow,
Or prosper, but by that same tree
It clings about; so I by Thee.
What need I then to feare at all,
So long as I about Thee craule?
But if that Tree sho'd fall, and die,
Tumble shall heav'n, and down will I.

---

[9] Cf. Cowper (end of "Task")
    "Whose approbation prospers even mine."

His wish to God.

I WOULD to God, that mine old age might have
    Before my last, but here a living grave,
Some one poore Almes-house; there to lie, or stir,
Ghost-like, as in my meaner sepulcher;
A little piggin,[1] and a pipkin[2] by,
To hold things fitting my necessity;
Which, rightly us'd, both in their time and place,
Might me excite to fore and after-grace.
Thy Crosse, my *Christ*, fixt 'fore mine eyes sho'd be,
Not to adore that, but to worship Thee.
So, here the remnant of my dayes I'd spend,
Reading Thy Bible, and my Book;[3] *so end.*

Satan.

WHEN we 'gainst Satan stoutly fight, the more
    He teares and tugs us, then he did before; [*than*
Neglecting once to cast a frown on those
Whom ease makes his, without the help of blowes.

---

[1] =earthenware dish=a little pig—still its name:=also a wooden half-barrel pail having one stave longer than the rest to serve as handle.

[2] =a little tiny earthen pot with handle of same. See Glossarial Index.   [3] i. e. the Bible, which is my book.

Hell.

HELL is no other, but a soundlesse[4] pit,
    Where no one beame of comfort peeps in it.

The way.

WHEN I a ship see on the Seas,
    Cuft with those watrie savages,
And therewithall, behold, it hath
In all that way no beaten path;
Then, with a wonder, I confesse,
Thou art our way i'th wildernesse:
And while we blunder in the dark,
Thou art our candle there, or spark.

Great grief, great glory.

THE lesse our sorrowes here and suffrings cease,
    The more our Crownes of Glory there increase.

Hell.

HELL is the place where whipping-cheer abounds,
    But no one Jailor there to wash the wounds.[5]

---

[4] =fathomless.
[5] Cf. Acts of the Apostles of the jailor at Philippi: c. xvi. 33.

The Bell-man.

ALONG the dark, and silent night,
   With my Lantern, and my Light,
And the tinkling of my Bell,
Thus I walk, and this I tell:
Death and dreadfulnesse call on,
To the gen'rall Session;
To whose dismall Barre, we there
All accompts must come to cleere:
Scores of sins w'ave made here many,
Wip't out few, (God knowes) if any.
Rise, ye Debters, then, and fall
To make paiment, while I call.
Ponder this, when I am gone;
By the clock 'tis almost *One.*

The goodnesse of his God.

WHEN Winds and Seas do rage,
   And threaten to undo me,
Thou dost their wrath asswage,
   If I but call unto Thee.

A mighty storm last night
   Did seek my soule to swallow,
But by the peep of light
   A gentle calme did follow.

What need I then despaire,
  Though ills stand round about me;
Since mischiefs neither dare
  To bark, or bite, without Thee?

The Widdowes teares: or, Dirge of Dorcas.

1. COME pitie us, all ye, who see
   Our Harps hung on the Willow-tree:
Come pitie us, ye Passers by,
Who see, or heare poor Widdowes crie:
Come pitie us; and bring your eares,
And eyes, to pitie Widdowes teares.
  Chor. And when you are come hither;
      Then we will keep
      A Fast, and weep
    Our eyes out all together.

2. For *Tabitha*, who dead lies here,
  Clean washt, and laid out for the Beere;
O modest Matrons, weep and waile!
For now the Corne and Wine must faile:
The Basket and the Bynn of Bread,
Wherewith so many soules were fed
  Chor. Stand empty here for ever:
      And ah! the Poore,
      At thy worne Doore,
Shall be releevèd never.

3. Woe worth the Time, woe worth the day,
   That reav'd us of thee *Tabitha* !
   For we have lost, with thee, the Meale,
   The Bits, the Morsells, and the deale[6]
   Of gentle Paste, and yeelding Dow,
   That Thou on Widdowes didst bestow.
   Chor. All's gone, and Death hath taken
       Away from us
       Our Maundie ;[7] thus,
   Thy Widdowes stand forsaken.

4. Ah *Dorcas, Dorcas !* now adieu
   We bid the Creuse and Pannier too :
   I and the flesh, for and[8] the fish,
   Dol'd to us in That Lordly dish.
   We take our leaves now of the Loome,
   From whence the house-wives cloth did come :
   Chor. The web affords now nothing ;
       Thou being dead,
       The woosted[9] thred
   Is cut, that made us clothing.

---

[6] = the portion dealt out.   [7] See Glossarial Index s. v.

[8] 'for and': an old and originally perhaps intransitive form of 'and' or 'also,' but sometimes, as here, used simply as 'and.'

[9] = worsted.

5. Farewell the Flax and Reaming[1] wooll,
With which thy house was plentifull.
Farewell the Coats, the Garments, and
The Sheets, the Rugs, made by thy hand.
Farewell thy Fier and thy Light,
That ne're went out by Day or Night :
  Chor. No, or thy zeale so speedy,
      That found a way
      By peep of day,
  To feed and cloth the Needy.

6. But, ah, alas! the Almond Bough,
And Olive Branch is wither'd now.
The Wine Presse now is ta'ne from us,
The Saffron and the Calamus.[2]
The Spice and Spiknard hence is gone,
The Storax and the Cynamon,
  Chor. The Caroll of our gladnesse
      Ha's taken wing,
      And our late spring
  Of mirth is turn'd to sadnesse.[3]

---

[1] = *mantling*, or like wine poured out: hence here picturesquely applied to wool carded into long locks ready for thread making.

[2] = a gum from the calamus odoratus or aromaticus.

[3] Exodus xxx. 23.

7. How wise wast thou in all thy waies!
How worthy of respect and praise!
How Matron-like didst thou go drest!
How soberly above the rest
Of those that prank[4] it with their Plumes;
And jet[5] it with their choice purfumes.
  Chor. Thy vestures were not flowing:
     Nor did the street
     Accuse thy feet
  Of mincing[6] in their going.

8. And though thou here li'st dead, we see
A deale[7] of beauty yet in thee.
How sweetly shewes thy smiling face,
Thy lips with all diffusèd grace!
Thy hands (though cold) yet spotlesse, white,
And comely as the Chrysolite.
  Chor. Thy belly like a hill is,
     Or as a neat
     Cleane heap of wheat,
  All set about with Lillies.

[4] = adorn: but generally used in an ill sense as over-adorn, or adorn ostentatiously and fantastically. [5] = to throw one's body or one's self forward, i. e. to strut proudly. Cf. Glossarial Index s. v.

[6] = walking in a proud fantastic or affected manner. See Isaiah iii. 16, where margin has 'walking nicely' (i. e. delicately).

[7] See Glossarial Index under 'deale.'

9. Sleep with thy beauties here, while we
Will shew these garments made by thee;
These were the Coats, in these are read
The monuments of *Dorcas* dead.
These were thy Acts, and thou shalt have
These hung, as honours o're thy Grave:
Chor. And after us (distressèd)
   Sho'd fame be dumb;
  Thy very Tomb
 Would cry out, *Thou art blessèd.*

To God, in time of plundering.

RAPINE has yet tooke nought from me;
 But if it please my God, I be
Brought at the last to th' utmost bit,
God make me thankfull still for it.
I have been gratefull for my store:
Let me say grace when there's no more.

To his Saviour. The New-yeers gift.

THAT little prettie bleeding part
 Of Foreskin send to me:
And Ile returne a bleeding Heart,
 For New-yeers gift to Thee.

> Rich is the Jemme that Thou did'st send,
>   Mine's faulty too, and small:
> But yet this Gift Thou wilt commend,
>   Because I send Thee *all*.

Doomes-Day.

> LET not that Day Gods Friends and Servants scare:
> The Bench is then their place; and not the Barre

The Poores Portion.

> THE sup'rabundance of my store,
>   That is the portion of the poore:
> Wheat, Barley, Rie, or Oats; what is't
> But he takes tole of? all the Griest.[s]
> Two raiments have I: *Christ* then makes
> This Law; that He and I part stakes.
> Or have I two loaves; then I use
> The poore to cut, and I to chuse.

The White Island: or place of the Blest.

> IN this world (the *Isle of Dreames*)
>   While we sit by sorrowes streames,
> Teares and terrors are our theames
>   Reciting:

---

[s] = grist.

But when once from hence we flie,
More and more approaching nigh
Unto young Eternitie
                Uniting :

In that *whiter Island*, where
Things are evermore sincere ;[9]
Candor[10] here, and lustre there
                Delighting :

There no monstrous fancies shall
Out of hell an horrour call,
To create (or cause at all)
                Affrighting.

There in calm and cooling sleep
We our eyes shall never steep ;
But eternall watch shall keep,
                Attending

Pleasures, such as shall pursue
Me immortaliz'd, and you ;
And fresh joyes, as never too
                Have ending.

See Glossarial Index s. v.   [10] = whiteness.

To Christ.

I CRAWLE, I creep; my *Christ*, I come
   To Thee, for curing *Balsamum:*
Thou hast, nay more, Thou art the Tree,
Affording salve of Soveraigntie.
My mouth I'le lay unto Thy wound
Bleeding, that no Blood touch the ground:
For, rather then one drop shall fall   [*than*
To wast, my JESU, I'le take all.

To God.

GOD! to my little meale and oyle,
   Add but a bit of flesh, to boyle:
And Thou my Pipkinnet[1] shalt see,
Give a *wave-offring* unto Thee.

Free Welcome.

GOD He refuseth no man; but makes way
   For All that now come, or hereafter may.

Gods Grace.

GODS Grace deserves here to be daily fed,
   That, thus increast, it might be perfected.

---

[1] Diminutive of 'pipkin.'

Coming to Christ.

TO him, who longs unto his CHRIST to go,
    Celerity even it self is slow.

Correction.

GOD had but one Son free from sin; but none
    Of all His sonnes free from correction.[2]

Gods Bounty.

GOD, as He's potent, so He's likewise known,
    To give us more then Hope can fix upon. [*than*

Knowledge.

SCIENCE in God, is known to be
    A Substance, not a Qualitie.

Salutation.

CHRIST, I have read, did to His Chaplains say,
    Sending them forth, *Salute no man by th' way*:[3]
Not, that He taught His Ministers to be
Unsmooth, or sowre, to all civilitie;

---

[2] A favorite saying with the old Puritan Preachers.
[3] The elaborateness of Eastern salutations, wherein much time was consumed, explains the injunction.

But to instruct them, to avoid all snares
Of tardidation[4] in the Lords Affaires.
Manners are good : but till his errand ends,
Salute we must, nor Strangers, Kin, or Friends.

Lasciviousnesse.

LASCIVIOUSNESSE is known to be
    The sister to saturitie.[5]

Teares.

GOD from our eyes all teares hereafter wipes,
    And gives His Children kisses then, not stripes.

Gods Blessing.

IN vain our labours are, whatsoe're they be,
    Unlesse God gives the *Benedicite*.

God, and Lord.

GOD, is His Name of Nature ; but that word
    Implies His Power, *when He's cal'd the LORD*.

The Judgment-Day.

GOD hides from man the reck'ning Day, that He
    May feare it ever for uncertaintie :

---

[4] = delaying.   [5] Probably used with the double sense of the Latin *saturitas* = excess and ordure.

That being ignorant of that one, he may
Expect the coming of it ev'ry day.

Angells.

ANGELLS are callèd Gods; yet of them, none
   Are Gods, but by *participation :*
As just Men are intitled Gods, yet none
Are Gods, of them, but by Adoption.

Long life.

THE longer thred of life we spin,
   The more occasion still to sin.

Teares.

THE teares of Saints more sweet by farre,
   Then all the songs of sinners are.   [*than*

Manna.

THAT Manna, which God on His people cast,
   Fitted it self to ev'ry Feeders tast.

Reverence.

TRUE rev'rence is (as *Cassiodore*[6] doth prove)
   The feare of God, commixt with cleanly love.

---

[6] Reverentia est enim Domini timor cum amore permixtus : (Cassiodor. Expos. in Psalt. xxxiv. 30. p. 118.)

Mercy.

MERCY, the wise Athenians held to be
    Not an Affection, but a *Deitie*.

Wages.

AFTER this life, the wages shall
    Not shar'd alike be unto all.

Temptation.

GOD tempteth no one (as S. *Aug'stine* saith)[7]
    For any ill; but, for the proof of Faith:
Unto temptation God exposeth some;
But none, of purpose, to be overcome.

Gods hands.

GODS hands are round, & smooth, that gifts may fall
Freely from them, and hold none back at all.

Labour.

LABOUR we must, and labour hard
    I'th *Forum* here, or *Vineyard*.

---

[7] Cf. Serm. ii De tentatione Abrahamae a Deo—"Deus tentat ut aperiat homini," and again, "Deus tentat ut doceat:" (Op. v. pp. 5, 7, *et alibi*.

Mora Sponsi, *the stay of the Bridegroome.*

THE time the Bridegroom stayes from hence,
  Is but the time of penitence.

Roaring.

ROARING is nothing but a weeping part,
  Forc'd from the mighty dolour of the heart.

The Eucharist.

HE that is hurt seeks help: sin is the wound;
  The salve for this i'th Eucharist is found.

Sin severely punisht.

GOD in His own Day will be then severe,
  To punish great sins, who small faults whipt
    here.

Montes Scripturarum, *the Mounts of the Scriptures.*

THE Mountains of the Scriptures are (some say)
  Moses, and *Iesus*, callèd *Joshua:*
The *Prophets*, Mountains of the Old are meant;
The *Apostles*, Mounts of the *New Testament*.

Prayer.

A PRAYER, that is said alone,
    Starves, having no companion.
Great things ask for, when thou dost pray,
And those great are, which ne're decay.
Pray not for silver, rust eats this;
Ask not for gold, which metall is:
Nor yet for houses, which are here
But earth: *such vowes nere reach Gods eare.*

Christs sadnesse.

CHRIST was not sad, i'th garden, for His own
    Passion, but for His sheeps dispersion.

God heares us.

GOD, who's in Heav'n, will hear from thence;
    If not to'th sound, yet, to the sense.

God.

GOD (as the learnèd *Damascen*[8] doth write)
    A *Sea of Substance* is, *Indefinite.*

---

[8] Ioann. Damasc. de Fide Orthod. i. 9: (Op. i. p. 142 Lequier.

Clouds.

HE that ascended in a cloud, shall come
   In clouds, descending to the publike *Doome*.[9]

Comforts in contentions.

THE same, who crownes the Conquerour, will be
   A Coadjutor in the Agonie.

Heaven.

HEAV'N is most faire; but fairer He
   That made that fairest Canopie.

God.

IN God there's nothing, but 'tis known to be
   Ev'n God Himself, in perfect *Entitie*.

His Power.

GOD can do all things, save but what are known
   For to imply a contradiction.

Christs words on the Crosse, My God, My God.

CHRIST, when He hung the dreadfull Crosse
     upon,
Had (as it were) a *Dereliction*;

---

[9] See Glossarial Index s. v.

In this regard, in those great terrors He
Had no one *Beame* from Gods sweet Majestie.

Jehovah.

JEHOVAH, as *Boëtius*[1] saith,
   No number of the *Plurall* hath.

Confusion of face.

GOD then confounds mans face, when He not hears
The Vowes of those, who are Petitioners.

Another.

THE shame of mans face is no more [than
   Then prayers repel'd, (sayes *Cassiodore*.)[2]

Beggars.

JACOB Gods Beggar was; and so we wait
   (Though ne're so rich) all beggars at His Gate.

---

[1] Nulla est omnino pluralitas, quare nec numerus (Boetius de Trin. ii. p. 1251 : Migne.)

[2] Fideles *non erubescunt*, quoniam impetrant. *Erubescere* enim decepti est, qui ad sua desideria non valet pervenire : (Cassiod : Expos. in Psalt. xxxiii. 5, p. 110).

Good, and bad.

THE Bad among the Good are here mixt ever:
  The Good without the Bad are here plac'd never.

Sin.

SIN *no existence ; Nature none it hath,*
  Or Good at all, (as learn'd *Aquinas* saith.)[3]

Martha, Martha.

THE repetition of the name made known
  No other, then *Christs* full Affection. [*than*

Youth, and Age.

GOD on our Youth bestowes but little ease ;
  But on our Age most sweet *Indulgences.*

Gods Power.

GOD is so potent, as His Power can
  Draw out of *bad* a soveraigne *good* to man.

Paradise.

PARADISE is (as from the Learn'd I gather)
  A quire of blest Soules circling in the Father.

---

[3] See St. Thomas contra Gentes, l. iii, c. 7, and De Malo Q. i. a. i. u. 20.

Observation.

THE Jewes, when they built Houses (I have read)
    One part thereof left still unfinishèd :
To make them, thereby, mindfull of their own
Cities most sad and dire destruction.[4]

The Asse.

GOD did forbid the Israelites, to bring
    An Asse unto Him, for an *offering :*
Onely, by this dull creature, to expresse
His detestation to all slothfulnesse.

Observation.

THE Virgin-Mother stood at distance (there)
    From her Sonnes Crosse, not shedding once a
    teare :
Because the Law forbad to sit and crie
For those, who did as malefactors die.

---

[4] "The Jews at this day, when they build a house, they are, say the Rabbins, to leave one part of it unfinished, and lying rude, in remembrance that Jerusalem and the temple are, at present, desolate (Hist. of Rites of Jews, by Leo Moden). At least they used to leave about a yard square of the house unplastered, on which they write in great letters that of the Psalmist, If I forget Jerusalem, then let my right hand forget her cunning (Ps. cxxxvii.) or else these words, Zecher Lechorbon, The Memory of the Desolation." (TRAPP on Nehemiah ii. 3 : 1656).

So she, to keep her mighty woes in awe,
Tortur'd her love, not to transgresse the Law.
Observe we may, how *Mary Joses* then,
And th' other *Mary (Mary Magdalen)*
Sate by the Grave; and sadly sitting there,
Shed for their Master many a bitter teare:
But 'twas not till their *dearest Lord* was dead;
And then to weep they both were licensèd.

Tapers.

THOSE Tapers, which we set upon the grave,
   In fun'rall pomp, but this importance[5] have;
That soules departed are not put out quite;
But, as they walk't here in their *vestures* white,
So live in Heaven, in everlasting light.

Christs Birth.

ONE Birth our Saviour had; the like none yet
   Was, or will be a *second* like to it.

The Virgin Mary.

TO work a *wonder*, God would have her shown,
   At once, a Bud, and yet a *Rose full-blowne.*

---

[5] Apparently used in sense of 'import.'

Another.

AS sun-beames pierce the glasse, and streaming in,
   No crack or Schisme leave i'th subtill skin:
So the Divine Hand work't, and brake no thred,
But, in a *Mother*, kept a *maiden-head*.

God.

GOD, in the *holy Tongue*, they call
   The Place that filleth *All in all*.

Another of God.

GOD'S said to leave this place, and for to come
   Nearer to that place, then to other some:
Of locall motion, in no least respect,
But only by impression of effect.

Another.

GOD is *Jehovah* cal'd; which name of His
   Implies or *Essence*, or the *He* that Is.

Gods presence.

GOD'S evident, and may be said to be
   Present with just men, to the veritie:

But with the wicked if He doth comply,
'Tis (as S. *Bernard* saith)[6] but seemingly.

Gods Dwelling.

GOD'S said to dwell there, wheresoever He
    Puts down some prints of His high Majestie:
As when to man He comes, and there doth place
His *holy Spirit*, or doth plant His *Grace*.

The Virgin Mary.

THE *Virgin Marie* was (as I have read)
    The House of God, by *Christ* inhabited;
Into the which He enter'd: but, the Doore
Once shut, was never to be open'd more.[7]

---

[6] 'Comply': probably in sense of French complaire, conform, or apply Himself to the humours of. The thought is frequent in St. Bernard. See under Balaam, etc.

[7] The reference is to Ezekiel xliv. 2, which is applied to the Virgin Mary in the Roman Breviary. Off. Conc. See St. Bernard (Op. iii. p. 813: Venet: 1727), or rather Bernard (of Toledo) to whom the work belongs, though it was formerly attributed to Bernard of Clairvaux—"Tu es castellum in quod Iesus intravit, habens turrim humilitatis, &c.

To God.

GOD'S undivided, *One* in *Persons Three*;
  And *Three* in *Inconfusèd Unity*:
Originall of Essence there is none,
'Twixt God the *Father, Holy Ghost*, and *Sonne*:
And though the *Father* be the first of *Three*,
'Tis but by *Order*, not by *Entitie*.

Upon Woman and Mary.

SO long (it seem'd) as *Maries* Faith was small,
  Christ did her *Woman*, not her *Mary* call:
But no more *Woman*, being strong in Faith;
But *Mary* cal'd then (as S. *Ambrose* saith.)[8]

North and South.

THE *Jewes* their beds, and offices of ease,
  Plac't *North* and *South*, for these cleane pur-
    poses;
That mans uncomely froth might not molest
Gods wayes and walks, which lie still East and West.

---

[8] See Expos. in. Luc. Lib. x. 161 sq: (Op. i. p. 1539 edn. Bened. Paris 1686.)

Sabbaths.

SABBATHS are threefold, (as S. *Austine* sayes :)[9]
 The first of Time, or Sabbath here of Dayes;
The second is a Conscience trespasse-free;
The last the *Sabbath of Eternitie*.

The Fast, or Lent.

NOAH the first was (as Tradition sayes)
 That did ordaine the Fast of forty Dayes.[1]

Sin.

THERE is no evill that we do commit,
 But hath th' extraction of some good from it:
As when we sin; God, the great *Chymist*, thence
Drawes out th' *Elixar*[2] of true penitence.

God.

GOD is more here, then in another place, [*than*
 Not by His *Essence*, but commerce of *Grace*.

---

[9] See *de Civititate Dei*, xxii. 30: (Op. vii. p. 701): also on the 'conscience trespasse free' Enarr. in Ps. xci. 1, and St. Jerome in Ezech. xlvi. 1, apud a-Lapide *in locum*.

[1] St. Augustine (Serm. 69) compares together Lent and the Deluge. So, too, St. Ambrose (*de Jejunio*) and Origen.

[2] = elixir.

This, and the next World.

GOD hath this world for many made; 'tis true:
But He hath made the world to come for few.[3]

Ease.

GOD gives to none so absolute an Ease,
　　As not to know, or feel some *Grievances*.

Beginnings and Endings.

PAUL, he began ill, but he ended well;
　Judas began well, but he foulely fell:
In godlinesse, not the beginnings, so
Much as the ends are to be lookt unto.

Temporall Goods.

THESE temp'rall goods God (the most Wise) commends
To th' good and bad, in common, for two ends:
First, that these goods none here may o're esteem,
Because the wicked do partake of them:

---

[3] One must take every opportunity of protesting against this perversion of Divine Truth. The vision of the Apocalypse—1900 years ago—was not of 'few' but of an unreckonable multitude.

Next, that these ills none cowardly may shun;
Being, oft here, the just mans portion.

Hell fire.

THE fire of Hell this strange condition hath,
    To burn, not shine (as learnèd *Basil* saith.)[4]

Abels *Bloud.*

SPEAK, did the Bloud of *Abel* cry
    To God for vengeance; yes, say I;
Ev'n as the sprinkled bloud cal'd on
God, for an expiation.

Another.

THE bloud of *Abel* was a thing
    Of such a rev'rend reckoning,
As that the old World thought it fit,
Especially to sweare by it.

A Position in the Hebrew Divinity.

ONE man repentant is of more esteem
    With God, then one, that never sin'd 'gainst
        Him. [5]   [*than*

---

[4] See a very striking passage in St. Basil Hom. on Psalm xxviii: (Op. i. p. 121, edn. Garnier).

[5] Questionable exegesis of (I suppose) Talmudic origin.

Penitence.

THE Doctors, in the Talmud, say,
   That in this world, one onely day
In true repentance spent, will be
More worth, then Heav'ns Eternitie.   [*than*

God's presence.

GOD'S present ev'ry where; but most of all
   Present by Union *Hypostaticall*:[6]
God, He is there, where's nothing else (Schooles say)
And nothing else is there, *where He's away*.

The Resurrection possible, and probable.

FOR each one Body, that i'th earth is sowne,
   There's an up-rising but of one for one:
But for each Graine, that in the ground is thrown,
Threescore or fourescore spring up thence for one:
So that the wonder is not halfe so great,
Of ours, as is the rising of the wheat.

Christs Suffering.

JUSTLY our *dearest Saviour* may abhorre us,
   Who hath more suffer'd by us farre, then for us.
                                      [*than*

[6] = substantially.

Sinners.

SINNERS confounded are a twofold way,
   Either as when (the learnèd Schoolemen say)
Mens sins destroyed are, when they repent;
Or when, for sins, men suffer punishment.

Temptations.

NO man is tempted so, but may o'recome,
   If that he has a will to Masterdome.

Pittie, and punishment.

GOD doth embrace the good with love; & gaines
   The good by mercy, as the bad by paines.

Gods price, and mans price.

GOD bought man here with his hearts blood
      expence;
And man sold God here for base *thirty pence*.

Christs Action.

CHRIST never did so great a work, but there
   His humane Nature did, in part, appeare:
Or, ne're so meane a peece, but men might see
Therein some beames of His Divinitie:

So that, in all He did, there did combine
His Humane Nature, and His Part Divine.

Predestination.

PREDESTINATION is the Cause alone
   Of many standing, but of fall to none.

Another.

ART thou not destin'd? then, with hast, go on
   To make thy faire *Predestination:*
If thou canst change thy life, God then will please
To change, or call back, His past *Sentences.*

Sin.

SIN never slew a soule, unlesse there went
   Along with it some tempting blandishment.

Another.

SIN is an act so free, that if we shall
   Say,[7] 'tis not free, 'tis then no sin at all.

---

[7] Not to '*say*' but actually to be '*not free.*' The meaning perhaps is that sin is so free that we are never constrained to it, but if we say that is believe of a thing that we are constrained to it or commanded to do it, then is it no sin.

Another.

SIN is the cause of death; and sin's alone
   The cause of Gods *Predestination:*
And from Gods *Prescience* of mans sin doth flow
Our *Destination* to eternall woe.

Prescience.

GODS *Prescience makes none sinfull;* but th'
   offence
Of man's the chief cause of Gods *Prescience.*

Christ.

TO all our wounds, here, whatsoe're they be,
   Christ is the one sufficient *Remedie.*

Christs Incarnation.

CHRIST took our Nature on Him, not that He
   'Bove all things lov'd it, for the puritie:
No, but He drest Him with our humane Trim,
Because our flesh stood most in need of Him.

Heaven.

HEAVEN is not given for our good works here:
   Yet it is given to the *Labourer.*

Gods keyes.

GOD has *foure keyes*, which He reserves alone;
　The first of *Raine*, the key of *Hell* next known
With the third key He opes and shuts the wombe;
And with the *fourth key* He unlocks the tombe.[8]

Sin.

THERE'S no constraint to do amisse,
　Whereas but one enforcement is.

Almes.

GIVE unto all, lest he, whom thou deni'st,
　May chance to be no other man, but *Christ*.

Hell fire.

ONE onely fire has Hell; but yet it shall,
　Not after one sort, there excruciate all:
But look, how each transgressor onward went
Boldly in sin, shall feel more punishment.

To keep a true Lent.

1. IS this a Fast, to keep
　　　The Larder leane?
　　　　　And cleane
　From fat of Veales, and Sheep?

---

[8] Rabbinical lore.

2. Is it to quit the dish
      Of Flesh, yet still
            To fill
The platter high with Fish?

3. Is it to fast an houre,
      Or rag'd [9] to go,
            Or show
A down-cast look, and sowre?

4. No: 'tis a Fast, to dole
      Thy sheaf of wheat,
            And meat,
Unto the hungry Soule.

5. It is to fast from strife,
      From old debate,
            And hate;
To circumcise thy life.

6. To shew a heart grief-rent;
      To sterve thy sin,
            Not Bin;
And that's to keep thy Lent.

[9] = ragged.

No time in Eternitie.

BY houres we all live here, in Heaven is known
    No spring of Time, or Times succession.

His Meditation upon Death.

BE those few hours, which I have yet to spend,
    Blest with the Meditation of my end :
Though they be few in number, I'm content ;
If otherwise, I stand indifferent :
Nor makes it matter, *Nestors* yeers to tell,
If man lives long, and if he live not well.
A multitude of dayes still heapèd on,
Seldome brings order, but confusion.
Might I make choice, long life sho'd be withstood ;
Nor wo'd I care how short it were, if good :
Which to effect, let ev'ry passing Bell
Possesse my thoughts,[1] next comes my dolefull knell :
And when the night perswades me to my bed,
I'le thinke I'm going to be buried :
So shall the Blankets which come over me,
Present those Turfs, which once[2] must cover me :

---

[1] i. e. Possesse my thoughts [that] next, &c.
[2] See Glossarial Index s. v.

And with as firme behaviour I will meet
The sheet I sleep in, as my Winding-sheet.
When sleep shall bath his body in mine eyes,
I will believe, that then my body dies:
And if I chance to wake, and rise thereon,
I'le have in mind my Resurrection,
Which must produce[3] me to that *Gen'rall Doome*,
To which the Pesant,[4] so the Prince must come,
To heare the Judge give sentence on the Throne,
Without the least hope of affection.[5]
Teares, at that day, shall make but weake defence;
When Hell and Horrour fright the Conscience.
Let me, though late, yet at the last, begin
To shun the least Temptation to a sin;
Though to be tempted be no sin, untill
Man to th' alluring object gives his will.
Such let my life assure me, when my breath
Goes theeving from me, I am safe in death;
Which is the height of comfort, when I fall,
I rise triumphant in my Funerall.

Cloaths for Continuance.

THOSE Garments lasting evermore,
    Are works of mercy to the poore,

---

[3] = lead me forth.   [4] = peasant.   [5] = partiality.

Which neither Tettar,[6] Time, or Moth
Shall fray that silke, or fret this cloth.

To God.

COME to me God; but do not come
    To me, as to the gen'rall Doome,
In power; or come Thou in that state,
When Thou Thy Lawes didst promulgate,
Whenas the Mountains quak'd for dread,
And sullen clouds bound up his head.
No, lay thy stately terrours by,
To talke with me familiarly;
For if Thy thunder-claps I heare,
I shall lesse swoone, then die for feare.   [*than*
Speake Thou of love and I'le reply
By way of *Epithalamie*,
Or sing of *mercy*, and I'le suit
To it my Violl and my Lute:
Thus let Thy lips but love distill,
Then come my God, and hap what will.

The Soule.

WHEN once the Soule has lost her way,
    O then, how restlesse do's she stray!

---

[6] = worms that eat away cloth, for skin tetter (ringworm) was supposed to be due to a worm.

And having not her God for light,
How do's she erre[6] in endlesse night!

The Judgement-day.

IN doing justice, God shall then be known,
 Who shewing mercy here, few priz'd, or none.

Sufferings.

WE merit all we suffer, and by far
 More stripes, then God layes on the sufferer.

[*than*

Paine and pleasure.

GOD suffers not His Saints, and Servants deere,
 To have continuall paine, or pleasure here:
But look how night succeeds the day, so He
Gives them by turnes their grief and jollitie.

Gods presence.

GOD is *all-present* to whate're we do,
 And as *all-present*, so *all-filling* too.

Another.

THAT there's a God, we all do know,
 But what God is, we cannot show.

[6] = wander.

The poore mans part.

TELL me rich man, for what intent
   Thou load'st with gold thy vestiment?
Whenas the poore crie out, to us
Belongs all gold superfluous.

The right hand.

GOD has a Right Hand, but is quite bereft
   Of that, which we do nominate the Left.

The Staffe and Rod.

TWO instruments belong unto our God;
   The one a *Staffe* is, and the next a *Rod:*
That if the twig sho'd chance too much to smart,
The staffe might come to play the friendly part.

God sparing in scourging.

GOD still rewards us more then our desert : [*than*
   But when He strikes, He quarter-acts[7] His part.

Confession.

CONFESSION twofold is (as *Austine* sayes) [8]
   The first of *sin* is, and the next of *praise:*

---

[7] = diminishes his blow by three-fourths = strikes gently.
[8] *Confessions*, et alibi, frequenter.

If ill it goes with thee, thy faults confesse :
If well, then chant Gods praise with cheerfulnesse.

Gods descent.

GOD is then said for to descend, when He
    Doth, here on earth, some thing of novitie ;[9]
As when, in humane nature He works more
Then ever, yet, the like was done before.   [than

No coming to God without Christ.

GOOD and great God! how sho'd I feare
    To come to Thee, if *Christ* not there !
Co'd I but think, He would not be
Present, to plead my cause for me ;
To Hell I'd rather run, then I   [than
Wo'd see Thy Face, and He not by.

Another, to God.

THOUGH Thou beest all that *Active Love*,
    Which heats those ravisht Soules above ;
And though all joyes spring from the glance
Of Thy most winning countenance ;
Yet sowre and grim Thou'dst seem to me ;
If through my *Christ* I saw not Thee.

---

[9] = newness or novelty (novitas).

The Resurrection.

THAT *Christ* did die, the *Pagan* saith;
    But that He rose, that's *Christians* Faith.

Coheires.

WE are Coheires with *Christ;* nor shall His own
    Heire-ship be lesse, by our adoption:
The number here of Heires, shall from the state
Of His great *Birth-right* nothing derogate.

The number of two.

GOD hates the *Duall Number;* being known
    The lucklesse number of division:
And when He blest each sev'rall Day, whereon
He did His *curious operation;*
'Tis never read there (as the Fathers say)[1]
God blest His work done on the *second day:*
Wherefore two prayers ought not to be said,
Or by our selves, or from the Pulpit read.

Hardning of hearts.

GOD'S said our hearts to harden then,
    Whenas His grace not supples men.

---

[1] Origen, St. Augustine, St. Jerome and others on Genesis c. i.

The Rose.

BEFORE Mans fall, the Rose was born,
   (S. *Ambrose* says)[2] without the Thorn:
But, for Mans fault, then was the Thorn,
Without the fragrant Rose-bud, born;
But ne're the Rose without the Thorn.

Gods time must end our trouble.

GOD doth not promise here to man, that He
   Will free him quickly from his miserie;
But in His own time, and when He thinks fit,
Then He will give a happy end to it.

Baptisme.

THE strength of *Baptisme*, that's within;
   It saves the soule, by drowning sin.

Gold and Frankincense.

GOLD serves for Tribute to the King;
   The *Frankincense* for Gods Offring.[3]

---

[2] See Hexaem iii. 11: (I. p. 51) "Surrexerat ante floribus immixta, &c.

[3] i. e. offering to God.

To God.

GOD, who me gives a will for to repent;
   Will add a power, to keep me innocent;
That I shall ne're that trespasse recommit,
When I have done true Penance here for it.

The chewing the Cud.

WHEN well we speak, & nothing do that's good,
   We not divide the *Hoof*, but chew the *Cud:*
But when good words, by good works, have their proof,
We then both chew the *Cud*, and cleave the *Hoof*.[4]

Christs twofold coming.

THY former coming was to cure
   My soules most desp'rate *Calenture*;[5]
Thy second *Advent*, that must be
To heale my Earths infirmitie.

---

[4] Unclean in the first instance, clean in the second. Cf. Leviticus xi. 4.

[5] = a heat-fever among sailors in hot climates, attended with the fancy that the sea is the green fields of home, and in this sense peculiarly applicable here.

To God, his gift.

AS my little Pot doth boyle,
    We will keep this *Levell-Coyle;*[6]
That a *Wave,* and I will bring
To my God, a *Heave-offering.*

Gods Anger.

GOD can't be wrathfull; but we may conclude,
    Wrathfull He may be, by similitude :
God's wrathfull said to be, when He doth do
That without *wrath,* which wrath doth *force us* to.

Gods Commands.

IN Gods commands, ne're ask the reason why ;
    Let thy *obedience* be the best Reply.

To God.

IF I have plaid the *Truant,* or have here
    Fail'd in my part ; Oh ! Thou that art my *deare.*
My *mild,* my *loving Tutor, Lord and God !*
Correct my errors gently with Thy Rod.
I know, that faults will many here be found,
But where sin swells, there let Thy grace abound.

---

[6] See Glossarial Index s. v.

To God.

THE work is done; now let my *Lawrell* be
  Given by none, but by Thy selfe, to me :
That done, with Honour Thou dost me create
Thy *Poet*, and Thy *Prophet Lawreat*.

Good Friday: Rex Tragicus, *or Christ going
  to His Crosse.*

PUT off Thy Robe of *Purple*, then go on
  To the sad place of execution :
Thine houre is come ; and the Tormentor stands
Ready, to pierce Thy tender Feet, and Hands.
Long before this, the base, the dull, the rude,
Th' inconstant, and unpurgèd Multitude
Yawne for Thy coming ; some e're this time crie,
How He deferres, how loath He is to die !
Amongst this scumme, the Souldier, with his speare,
And that sowre Fellow, with his *vineger*,
His *spunge*, and *stick*, do ask why Thou dost stay?
So do the *Skurfe*[7] and *Bran*[8] too : Go Thy way,

---

[7] To accuse any of skin disease was a common reproach, and constantly applied to the lower classes as putting them in the same rank with the lowest of the low, with whom these diseases were common. Thus we have 'scab' and 'scroyles' (Les escronëlles, the King's evil) and as adjectives scald and scurvy. [8] = thin bark.

Thy way, Thou guiltlesse man, and satisfie
By Thine approach, each their beholding eye.
Not as a thief, shalt Thou ascend the mount,
But like a Person of some high account:
The *Crosse* shall be Thy *Stage;* and Thou shalt there
The spacious field have for Thy *Theater.*
Thou art that *Roscius,*[9] and that markt-out man,
That must this day act the Tragedian,
To wonder and affrightment: Thou art He,
Whom all the flux[1] of Nations comes to see;
Not those poor Theeves that act their parts with
    Thee:
Those act without regard, when once a *King,*
And *God,* as Thou art, comes to suffering.
No, No, this *Scene* from Thee takes life and sense,
And soule and spirit, plot and excellence.
Why then begin, great King! ascend Thy Throne,
And thence proceed, to act Thy Passion
To such an height, to such a period rais'd,
As Hell, and Earth, and Heav'n may stand amaz'd.
God, and good Angells guide Thee; and so blesse
Thee in Thy severall parts of bitternesse;

---

[9] Singular use of the player-name.   [1] = flow or flood.

That those, who see Thee nail'd unto the Tree,
May (though they scorn Thee) praise and pitie Thee.
And we (Thy Lovers) while we see Thee keep
The Lawes of Action, will both sigh, and weep;
And bring our Spices, to embalm Thee dead;
That done, wee'l see Thee sweetly buri**è**d.

His words to Christ, going to the Crosse.

WHEN Thou wast taken, Lord, I oft have read,
  All Thy Disciples Thee forsook, and fled.[2]
Let their example not a pattern be
For me to flie, but now to follow Thee.

Another, to his Saviour.

IF Thou beest taken, *God* forbid,
  I flie from Thee, as others did:
But if Thou wilt so honour me,
As to accept my companie,
I'le follow Thee, hap hap what shall,[3]
Both to the *Judge*, and *Judgment-Hall:*

---

[2] St. Matthew xxvi. 56.

[3] I delete comma (,) after 'hap'—the first is a verb, the second its substantive=happen what hap shall.

And, if I see Thee posted there,
To be all-flayd with whipping-cheere,[4]
I'le take my share ; or els, my God,
Thy stripes I'le kisse, or burn the *Rod*.

His Saviours words, going to the Crosse.

HAVE, have ye no regard, all ye
    Who passe this way, to pitie me,
Who am a man of miserie![5]

A man both bruis'd, and broke, and one
Who suffers not here for mine own,
But for my friends *transgression!*

Ah ! *Sions Daughters*, do not feare
The *Crosse*, the *Cords*, the *Nailes*, the *Speare*,
The *Myrrhe*, the *Gall*, the *Vineger*

For *Christ*, your loving Saviour, hath
Drunk up the wine of Gods fierce wrath ;
Onely, there's left a little froth,

---

[4] See Glossarial Index s. v.
[5] See Memorial-Introduction for parallel in George Herbert.

Lesse for to tast, then for to shew,   [*than*
What bitter cups had been your due,
Had He not drank them up for *you*.

His Anthem, to Christ on the Crosse.

WHEN I behold Thee, almost slain,
    With one, and all parts, full of
        pain :
When I Thy gentle Heart do see
Pierc't through, and dropping bloud, for
    me,
I'le call, and cry out, Thanks to Thee.

Vers. But yet it wounds my soule, to think,
    That for my sin, Thou, Thou must drink,
    Even Thou alone, the *bitter cup*
    Of *furie*, and of *vengeance* up.

Chor. Lord, I'le not see Thee to drink all
    The *Vineger*, the *Myrrhe*, the *Gall* :

Ver. Chor. But I will sip a little wine ;
    Which done, Lord say, *The rest is mine.*

This Crosse-Tree here
Doth JESUS *beare,*
Who sweet'ned first,
The Death accurs't.

HERE all things ready are, make hast, make hast away;
For long this work wil be, & very short this Day.
Why then, go on to act: Here's wonders to be done,
Before the last least sand of Thy ninth houre be run;
Or e're dark Clouds do dull, or dead the Mid-dayes Sun.

Act when Thou wilt,
Bloud will be spilt;
Pure Balm, that shall
Bring Health to All.
Why then, Begin
To powre first in
Some Drops of Wine,
In stead of Brine,
To search the Wound,
So long unsound:
And, when that's done,
Let Oyle, next, run,
To cure the Sore
Sinne made before.
And O! Deare Christ,
E'en as Thou di'st,
Look down, and see
Us weepe for Thee.
And tho (Love knows)
Thy dreadfull Woes
Wee cannot ease;
Yet doe Thou please,
Who Mercie art,
T'accept each Heart,
That gladly would
Helpe, if it could.
Meane while, let mee,
Beneath this Tree,
This Honour have,
To make my grave.

To his Saviours Sepulcher: his Devotion.

HAILE holy, and all-honour'd Tomb,
   By no ill haunted; here I come,
With shoes put off, to tread thy Roome.
I'le not prophane, by soile of sin,
Thy Doore, as I do enter in:
For I have washt both hand and heart,
This, that, and ev'ry other part;
So that I dare, with farre lesse feare,
Then full affection, enter here.   [*than*
Thus, thus I come to kisse Thy Stone
With a warm lip, and solemne one:
And as I kisse, I'le here and there
Dresse Thee with flowrie Diaper.
How sweet this place is! as from hence
Flow'd all *Panchaia's*[6] Frankincense;
Or rich *Arabia* did commix,
Here, all her rare *Aromaticks*.
Let me live ever here, and stir
No one step from this *Sepulcher*.
Ravisht I am! and down I lie,
Confus'd, in this brave Extasie.

[6] See Glossarial Index s. v.

Here let me rest ; and let me have
This for my *Heaven*, that was Thy *Grave:*
And, coveting no higher sphere,
I'le my Eternitie spend here.

His Offering, with the rest, at the Sepulcher.

TO joyn with them who here confer[7]
    Gifts to my Saviours Sepulcher ;
Devotion bids me hither bring
Somewhat for my Thank-Offering.
Loe ! thus I bring a Virgin-Flower,
To dresse my Maiden-Saviour.

His coming to the Sepulcher.

HENCE they have born my Lord ; behold ! the
    Stone
Is rowl'd away, and my sweet Saviour's gone.
Tell me, white[8] Angell, what is now become
Of Him we lately seal'd up in this Tombe ?
Is He, from hence, gone to the shades beneath,
To vanquish Hell, as here he conquer'd Death ?

---

[7] = bring together or in union.
[8] See Glossarial Index s. v.

If so, I'le thither follow, without feare,
And live in Hell, if that my *Christ* stayes there.

OF all the good things whatsoe're we do,
    God is the ΑΡΧΗ,[9] and the ΤΕΛΟΣ[10] too.

[9] = beginning.   [10] = end.

ALPHABETICAL INDEX OF FIRST LINES.

ALPHABETICAL INDEX OF FIRST LINES.

A.

	Vol.	Page
A Bachelour I will	i.	22
A christall Violl *Cupid* brought	ii.	200
A funerall stone	i.	50
A Golden Flie one shew'd to me	ii.	140
A *Gyges* Ring they beare about them still	ii.	248
A just man's like a Rock that turnes the wroth	ii.	81
A little mushroome-table spred	ii.	24
A little Saint best fits a little Shrine	ii.	246
A long-lifes-day I've taken paines	ii.	185
A Man prepar'd against all ills to come	ii.	40
A mans transgression God do's then remit	iii.	151
A master of a house (as I have read)	ii.	263
A prayer, that is said alone	iii.	188
A Rowle of Parchment *Clunn* about him beares	iii.	21
A sweet disorder in the dresse	i.	46
A wanton and lascivious eye	ii.	254
A way enchac't with glasse & beads	i.	156
A wearied Pilgrim, I have wandred here	iii.	75

	Vol.	Page
A willow Garland thou did'st send	ii.	97
About the sweet bag of a Bee	i.	51
Abundant plagues I late have had	iii.	142
Adverse and prosperous Fortunes both work on	iii.	135
Adversity hurts none, but onely such	ii.	229
Afflictions bring us joy in times to come	iii.	135
Afflictions they most profitable are	iii.	125
After true sorrow for our sinnes, our strife	iii.	157
After the Feast (my *Shapcot*) see	ii.	104
After the rare Arch-Poet JOHNSON dy'd	ii.	78
After this life, the wages shall	iii.	186
After thy labour take thine ease	iii.	86
Against diseases here the strongest fence	iii.	84
Ah *Ben!*	iii.	11
Ah *Biancha!* now I see	iii.	43
Ah, cruell Love! must I endure	i.	128
Ah my *Anthea!* Must my heart still break?	i.	40
Ah! my *Perilla!* do'st thou grieve to see	i.	14
Ah *Posthumus!* Our yeares hence flye	ii.	47
Ai me! I love, give him your hand to kisse	ii.	288
Alas! I can't, for tell me how	iii.	78
All are not ill Plots, that doe sometimes faile	iii.	81
All has been plundered from me, but my wit	ii.	286
All I have lost, that co'd bĕ rapt from me	iii.	170
All things are open to these two events	ii.	133
All things decay with Time: The Forrest sees	i.	38
All things o'r-rul'd are here by Chance	ii.	159
All things subjected are to Fate	ii.	179
Along, come along	iii.	63
Along the dark, and silent night	iii.	174

	Vol.	Page
Although our suffering meet with no reliefe	iii.	84
Although we cannot turne the fervent fit	iii.	146
Am I despis'd, because you say	i.	107
Among disasters that discention brings	ii.	265
Among these Tempests great and manifold	iii.	61
Among the *Mirtles*, as I walkt	ii.	3
Among thy Fancies, tell me this	ii.	43
And as time past when *Cato* the Severe	iii.	31
And, Cruell, Maid, because I see	i.	103
And must we part, because some say	i.	82
Angells are callèd Gods; yet of them, none	iii.	185
Angry if *Irene* be	ii.	170
An old, old widow *Greedy* needs wo'd wed	ii.	42
Anthea bade me tye her shooe	i.	23
Anthea I am going hence	ii.	294
Anthea laught, and fearing lest excesse	iii.	49
Apollo sings, his harpe resounds: give roome	iii.	109
Art quickens Nature; Care will make a face	i.	169
Art thou not destin'd? then, with hast, go on	iii.	202
As Gilly flowers do but stay	ii.	36
As *Julia* once a-slumb'ring lay	i.	121
As lately I a Garland bound	i.	167
As in our clothes, so likewise he who lookes	ii.	167
As oft as Night is banish'd by the Morne	i.	43
As shews the Aire, when with a Rain-bow grac'd	i.	68
As is your name, so is your comely face	iii.	43
As many Lawes and Lawyers do expresse	ii.	237
As my little Pot doth boyle	iii.	215
As sun-beames pierce the glasse, and streaming in	iii.	194

	Vol.	Page
As thou deserv'st, be proud; then gladly let	ii.	155
As wearied *Pilgrims*, once possest	ii.	190
Aske me what hunger is, and Ile reply	iii.	18
Aske me, why I do not sing	ii.	45
Aske me why I send you here	ii.	177
At Draw-Gloves we'l play	i.	172
At my homely Country-seat	ii.	83
At Post and Paire, or Slam, *Tom Tuck* would play	ii.	228
At Stool-ball, *Lucia*, let us play	ii.	226
Attempt the end, and never stand to doubt.	iii.	49
Away with silks, away with Lawn	ii.	85

B.

	Vol.	Page
Bacchus, let me drink no more	ii.	30
Bad are all surfeits; but Physitians call	iii.	6
Barre close as you can, and bolt fast too your doore	i.	169
Batt he gets children, not for love to reare 'em	i.	123
Be bold, my Booke, nor be abasht, or feare	ii.	185
Be not dismaide, though crosses cast thee downe	iii.	49
Be not proud, but now encline	i.	168
Be the Mistresse of my choice	ii.	216
Be those few hours, which I have yet to spend	iii.	206
Beauti's no other but a lovely Grace	ii.	289
Beauty, no other thing is, then a Beame	i.	55
Before Mans fall, the Rose was born	iii.	213
Before the Press scarce one co'd see	iii.	8
Beginne with *Jove*; then is the worke halfe done	ii.	39

	Vol.	Page
Begin to charme, and as thou stroak'st mine eares	i.	115
Begin with a kisse	ii.	242
Bell-man of Night, if I about shall go	iii.	134
Besides us two, i' th' Temple here's not one	ii.	110
Biancha, Let	i.	49
Bice laughs, when no man speaks; and doth protest	ii.	273
Bid me to live, and I will live	ii.	6
Bind me but to thee with thine haire	iii.	19
Blanch swears her Husband's lovely; when a scald	i.	55
Blessings, in abundance come	ii.	34
Blisse (last night drunk) did kisse his mothers knee	iii.	22
Boreman takes tole, cheats, flatters, lyes; yet *Boreman*	iii.	55
Borne I was to meet with Age	ii.	149
Born I was to be old	ii.	159
Both you two have	ii.	11
Break off Delay, since we but read of one	ii.	250
Breathe, *Julia*, breathe, and I'le protest	i.	119
Bright Tulips, we do know	ii.	138
Bring me my Rose-buds, Drawer come	ii.	178
Bring the holy crust of Bread	iii.	2
Brisk methinks I am, and fine	iii.	45
Broomsted a lamenesse got by cold and Beere	ii.	165
Brown bread *Tom Pennie* eates, and must of right	iii.	45
Buggins is Drunke all night, all day he sleepes	iii.	50

	Vol.	Page
Bungie do's fast; looks pale; puts Sack-cloth on	ii.	30
Burne, or drowne me, choose ye whether	ii.	255
Burr is a smell-feast, and a man alone	iii.	22
But borne, and like a short Delight	i.	120
By Dream I saw, one of the three	ii.	84
By houres we all live here, in Heaven is known	iii.	206
By so much, vertue is the lesse	ii.	254
By the next kindling of the day	ii.	283
By the weak'st means things mighty are o're-thrown	ii.	230
By those soft *Tods* of wooll	ii.	260
By Time, and Counsell, doe the best we can	ii.	27

C.

	Vol.	Page
Call me no more	ii.	67
Can I not come to Thee, my God, for these	iii.	139
Can I not sin, but thou wilt be	iii.	147
Care keepes the Conquest; 'tis no lesse renowne.	iii.	42
Case is a Lawyer, that near pleads alone	iii.	36
Center is known weak sighted, and he sells	ii.	85
Charm me asleep, and melt me so	i.	165
Charms, that call down the moon from out her sphere	i.	172
Cherrie-ripe, Ripe, Ripe, I cry	i.	33
Choose me your Valentine	i.	52
Christ, He requires still, wheresoere He comes	iii.	146
Christ, I have read, did to His Chaplains say	iii.	183
Christ never did so great a work, but there	iii.	201
Christ took our Nature on Him, not that He	iii.	203

	Vol.	Page
Christ was not sad, i'th garden, for His own	iii.	188
Christ, when He hung the dreadfull Crosse upon	iii.	189
Cleere are her eyes	ii.	153
Close keep your lips, if that you meane	ii.	248
Cob clouts his shooes, and as the story tells	ii.	207
Cock calls his Wife his Hen: when *Cock* goes too't	ii.	187
Come, *Anthea*, know thou this	ii.	223
Come *Anthea* let us two	ii.	256
Come blithefull Neatherds, let us lay.	ii.	235
Come bring your *sampler*, and with Art	i.	17
Come, bring with a noise	ii.	270
Come come away	ii.	55
Come down, and dance ye in the toyle	i.	15
Come guard this night the Christmas-Pie	ii.	271
Come, leave this loathèd Country-life, and then	ii.	116
Come pitie us, all ye, who see	iii.	175
Come, skilfull *Lupo*, now, and take	i.	65
Come sit we by the fires side	ii.	196
Come sit we under yonder Tree.	ii.	189
Come, Sons of Summer, by whose toile	i.	175
Come then, and like two Doves with silv'rie wings	ii.	173
Come thou not neere those men, who are like Bread	i.	11
Come thou, who art the Wine, and wit	ii.	146
Come to me God; but do not come	iii.	208
Come with the Spring-time forth Fair Maid, and be	ii.	60
Comely Acts well; and when he speaks his part	ii.	275

	Vol.	Page
Command the Roofe, great *Genius*, and from thence	ii.	239
Confession twofold is (as *Austine* sayes)	iii.	210
Conformity gives comelinesse to things	iii.	61
Conformity was ever knowne	i.	41
Conquer we shall, but we must first contend	iii.	19
Consider sorrowes, how they are aright	ii.	278
Consult ere thou begin'st, that done, go on	ii.	252
Crab faces gownes with sundry Furres; 'tis known	ii.	218
Craw cracks in sirrop; and do's stinking say	ii.	99
Crooked you are, but that dislikes not me	i.	172
Cuffe comes to church much; but he keeps his bed	i.	66
Cupid as he lay among	i.	84
Curse not the mice, no grist of thine they eat	ii.	62
Cynthius pluck ye by the eare	i.	89

D.

	Vol.	Page
Dead falls the Cause, if once the Hand be mute	ii.	31
Dean-bourn, farewell; I never look to see	i.	48
Deare *Perenna*, prethee come	i.	155
Deare, though to part it be a Hell	i.	56
Dearest of thousands, now the time drawes neere	ii.	195
Deer God	iii.	157
Despaire takes heart, when ther's no hope to speed	iii.	46
Dew sate on *Julia's* haire	ii.	132
Did I or love, or could I others draw	ii.	166
Die ere long, I'm sure, I shall	iii.	66

	Vol.	Page
Discreet and prudent we that Discord call	ii.	252
Display thy breasts, my *Julia*, there let me	i.	168
Doll she so soone began the wanton trade	ii.	77
Do's Fortune rend thee? Beare with thy hard Fate	ii.	282
Do with me, God! as Thou didst deal with *Iohn*	iii.	125
Down with the Rosemary and Bayes	iii.	4
Down with the Rosemary, and so	iii.	38
Dread not the shackles: on with thine intent	iii.	58
Drinke up	iii.	42
Drink Wine, and live here blithefull, while ye may	ii.	209
Droop, droop no more, or hang the head	i.	12
Drowning, drowning, I espie	iii.	33
Dry your sweet cheek, long drown'd with sorrows raine	ii.	1
Dull to my selfe, and almost dead to these	ii.	187
Dundrige his issue hath; but is not styl'd	ii.	156

E.

	Vol.	Page
Each must, in vertue, strive for to excell	ii.	28
Eaten I have; and though I had good cheere	ii.	159
Eeles winds and turnes, and cheats and steales; yet *Eeles*	ii.	84
E'ene all Religious courses to be rich	ii.	275
Empires of Kings, are now, and ever were	ii.	100
End now the White-loafe, & the Pye	iii.	6
Endym. Ah! *Lycidas*, come tell me why	ii.	136
Ere J goe hence and bee noe more	iii.	96

	Vol.	Page
Euc. Charon, O Charon, draw thy Boat to th' Shore	iii.	110
Every time seemes short to be	ii.	100
Evill no Nature hath; the losse of good	iii.	164
Examples lead us, and wee likely see	ii.	256
Excesse is sluttish: keepe the meane; for why?	iii.	82

F.

	Vol.	Page
Fain would I kisse my *Julia's* dainty Leg	ii.	59
Faire and foule dayes trip Crosse and Pile; The faire	ii.	145
Faire Daffadills, we weep to see	ii.	35
Faire pledges of a fruitfull Tree	ii.	124
Faire was the Dawne; and but e'ne now the Skies	i.	141
Faith is a thing that's four-square; let it fall	iii.	17
Fames pillar here, at last, we set	iii.	88
Farewell thou Thing, time-past so knowne, so deare	i.	76
Fat be my Hinde; unlearnèd be my wife	iii.	20
Feacie (some say) doth wash her clothes i'th' Lie	ii.	126
Fie, (quoth my Lady) what a stink is here?	ii.	184
Fight thou with shafts of silver, and o'rcome	i.	35
Fill me a mighty Bowle	ii.	209
Fill me my Wine in Christall; thus, and thus	ii.	142
First, *April*, she with mellow showrs	i.	38
First, for Effusions due unto the dead	i.	39
First, for your shape, the curious cannot shew	ii.	145
First, *Jollies* wife is lame; then next, loose-hipt	i.	107
First, may the hand of bounty bring	iii.	15

	Vol.	Page
First offer Incense, then thy field and meads	ii.	67
Fled are the Frosts, and now the Fields appeare	ii.	203
Flood, if he has for him and his a bit	iii.	83
Fly me not, though I be gray	ii.	154
Fly to my Mistresse, pretty pilfring Bee	i.	174
Fold now thine armes; and hang the head	i.	80
Fone sayes, those mighty whiskers he do's weare	i.	66
Fooles are they, who never know	i.	168
For all our workes, a recompence is sure	ii.	292
For all thy many courtesies to me	ii.	276
For being comely, consonant, and free	ii.	181
For brave comportment, wit without offence	iii.	24
For civill, cleane, and circumcisèd wit	ii.	154
For each one Body, that i'th earth is sowne	iii.	200
For my embalming, Julia, do but this	ii.	42
For my neighbour Ile not know	i.	145
For my part I never care	i.	141
For one so rarely tun'd to fit all parts	ii.	29
For punishment in warre, it will suffice	ii.	47
For ropes of pearle, first Madam *Vrsly* showes	ii.	217
For second course, last night, a Custard came	i.	80
For sport my *Julia* threw a Lace	ii.	20
For thirty yeares, *Tubbs* has been proud and poor	iii.	34
For Those my unbaptizèd Rhimes	iii.	119
For truth I may this sentence tell	iii.	66
Fortune did never favour one	ii.	149
Fortune no higher Project can devise	ii.	157
Fortune's a blind profuser of her own	ii.	226
Franck ne'r wore silk she sweares; but I reply	ii.	177

	Vol.	Page
Franck wo'd go scoure her teeth; and setting to't	ii.	243
Fresh strowings allow	ii.	257
Frollick Virgins once these were	ii.	82
From me my *Silvia* ranne away	iii.	10
From noise of Scare-fires rest ye free	ii.	28
From the dull confines of the drooping West	ii.	233
From the Temple to your home	ii.	197
From this bleeding hand of mine	i.	153

G.

	Vol.	Page
Gather ye Rose-buds while ye may	i.	144
Get up, get up for shame, the Blooming Morne	i.	116
Give house-roome to the best; *'Tis never known*	iii.	19
Give, if thou canst, an Almes; if not, afford	iii.	147
Give me a Cell	ii.	262
Give me a man that is not dull	iii.	60
Give me a reason why men call	ii.	286
Give me honours! what are these	iii.	145
Give me one kisse	ii.	157
Give me that man, that dares bestride	i.	51
Give me the food that satisfies a Guest	ii.	274
Give me wine, and give me meate	ii.	192
Give unto all, lest he, whom thou deni'st	iii.	204
Give *Want* her welcome if she comes; we find	ii.	186
Give way, and be ye ravisht by the Sun	ii.	157
Give way, give way, now, now my *Charles* shines here	ii.	224
Give way, give way ye Gates, and win	ii.	128
Glasco had none, but now some teeth has got	i.	78

FIRST LINES. 239

	Vol.	Page
Glasse, out of deepe, and out of desp'rate want	ii.	80
Glide, gentle streams, and beare	i.	72
Glory be to the Graces!	ii.	266
Glory no other thing is (*Tullie* sayes)	ii.	232
God, as He is most Holy knowne	iii.	125
God, as He's potent, so He's likewise known	iii.	183
God (as the learnèd *Damascen* doth write)	iii.	188
God bought man here with his hearts blood expence	iii.	201
God can do all things, save but what are known	iii.	189
God can't be wrathfull; but we may conclude	iii.	215
God co'd have made all rich, or all men poore	iii.	146
God did forbid the Israelites, to bring	iii.	192
God doth embrace the good with love; & gaines	iii.	201
God doth not promise here to man, that He	iii.	213
God from our eyes all teares hereafter wipes	iii.	184
God gives not onely corne, for need	iii.	146
God gives to none so absolute an Ease	iii.	198
God had but one Son free from sin; but none	iii.	183
God has a Right Hand, but is quite bereft	iii.	210
God has *foure keyes*, which He reserves alone	iii.	204
God has His whips here to a twofold end	iii.	126
God hates the *Duall Number*; being known	iii.	212
God hath this world for many made; 'tis true	iii.	198
God hath two wings, which He doth ever move	iii.	121
God heares us when we pray, but yet defers	iii.	127
God He refuseth no man; but makes way	iii.	182
God He rejects all Prayers that are sleight	iii.	123
God hides from man the reck'ning Day, that He	iii.	184
God in His own Day will be then severe	iii.	187

	Vol.	Page
God, in the *holy Tongue*, they call	iii.	194
God is above the sphere of our esteem	iii.	121
God is all fore-part; for, we never see	iii.	124
God is *all-present* to whate're we do	iii.	209
God is all-sufferance here; here He doth show	iii.	148
God, is His Name of Nature; but that word	iii.	184
God is *Jehovah* cal'd; which name of His	iii.	194
God is more here, then in another place	iii.	197
God is not onely mercifull, to call	iii.	124
God is not onely said to be	iii.	121
God is so potent, as His Power can	iii.	191
God is then said for to descend, when He	iii.	211
God loads, and unloads, (thus His work begins)	iii.	123
God makes not good men wantons, but doth bring	iii.	169
God n'ere afflicts us more then our desert	iii.	122
God on our Youth bestowes but little ease	iii.	191
God pardons those, who do through frailty sin	iii.	127
God scourgeth some severely, some He spares	iii.	124
God still rewards us more then our desert	iii.	210
God strikes His Church, but 'tis to this intent	iii.	127
God suffers not His Saints, and Servants deere	iii.	209
God tempteth no one (as S. *Aug'stine* saith)	iii.	186
God then confounds mans face, when He not hears	iii.	190
God! to my little meale and oyle	iii.	182
God when for sin He makes His Children smart	iii.	125
God when He's angry here with any one	iii.	121
God when He takes my goods and chattels hence	iii.	156

	Vol.	Page
God, who me gives a will for to repent	iii.	214
God, who's in Heav'n, will hear from thence	iii.	188
God will have all, or none; serve Him, or fall	iii.	141
Gods boundlesse mercy is (to sinfull man)	iii.	123
Gods Bounty, that ebbs lesse and lesse	iii.	149
God's evident, and may be said to be	iii.	194
Gods Grace deserves here to be daily fed	iii.	182
Gods hands are round, & smooth, that gifts may fall	iii.	186
Gods *Prescience makes none sinfull*; but th' offence	iii.	203
God's present ev'ry where; but most of all	iii.	200
Gods Rod doth watch while men do sleep, & then	iii.	125
God's said our hearts to harden then	iii.	212
God's said to dwell there, wheresoever He	iii.	195
God's said to leave this place, and for to come	iii.	194
God's undivided, *One* in *Persons Three*	iii.	196
Goddesse, I begin an Art	ii.	155
Goddesse, I do love a Girle	ii.	55
Goddesse of Youth, and Lady of the Spring	ii.	5
Go hence, and with this parting kisse	ii.	120
Go I must; when I am gone	ii.	162
Go on, brave *Hopton*, to effectuate that	iii.	47
Go prettie child, and beare this Flower	iii.	143
Go wooe young *Charles* no more to looke	ii.	187
Goe, happy Rose, and enterwove	i.	170
Goe hence away, and in thy parting know	iii.	109
Goe, perjur'd man; and if thou ere return	i.	84
Goe thou forth, my booke, though late	iii.	86
Goes the world now, it will with thee goe hard	i.	37

	Vol.	Page
Gold I have none, but I present my need	iii.	167
Gold I've none, for use or show	i.	153
Gold serves for Tribute to the King	iii.	213
Gone she is a long, long way	ii.	291
Good and great God! how sho'd I feare	iii.	211
Good day, *Mirtillo*. *Mirt*. And to you no lesse	i.	148
Good morrow to the day so fair	ii.	89
Good Precepts we must firmly hold	ii.	143
Good princes must be pray'd for : for the bad	i.	54
Good speed, for I this day	i.	150
Good things, that come of course, far lesse doe please	ii.	31
Great Cities seldome rest : If there be none	iii.	57
Great men by small meanes oft are overthrown	ii.	133
Grow for two ends, it matters not at all	ii.	217
Grow up in Beauty, as thou do'st begin	iii.	38
Groynes, for his fleshly *Burglary* of late	ii.	2
Grubs loves his Wife and Children, while that they	iii.	72
Grudgings turnes bread to stones, when to the Poore	ii.	196
Gryll eates, but ne're sayes Grace; to speak the troth	i.	82
Gubbs calls his children *Kitlings:* and wo'd bound	i.	138
Guesse cuts his shooes, and limping, goes about	i.	171

H.

Haile holy, and all-honour'd Tomb	iii.	222
Hanch, since he (lately) did interre his wife	ii.	290

	Vol.	Page
Hang up Hooks, and Sheers to scare	iii.	3
Hansome you are, and Proper you will be	iii.	28
Happily I had a sight	iii.	52
Happy's that man, to whom God gives	iii.	139
Hard are the two first staires unto a Crowne	iii.	17
Haste is unhappy; what we Rashly do	ii.	279
Hast thou attempted greatnesse? then go on	ii.	252
Hast thou begun an act? ne're then give o're	ii.	223
Have, have ye no regard, all ye	iii.	219
Have I not blest Thee? Then go forth; nor fear	ii.	86
Have ye beheld (with much delight)	ii.	102
He that ascended in a cloud, shall come	iii.	189
He that is hurt seeks help: sin is the wound	iii.	187
He that may sin, sins least; Leave to transgresse	ii.	8
He that will live of all cares dispossest	iii.	38
He that will not love, must be	i.	178
He who commends the vanquisht, speaks the Power	ii.	165
He, who has suffer'd Ship-wrack, feares to saile	ii.	184
He who wears Blacks, and mournes not for the Dead	iii.	62
Health is the first good lent to men	i.	71
Health is no other (as the learnèd hold)	ii.	224
Heare, ye Virgins, and Ile teach	ii.	27
Heav'n is most faire; but fairer He	iii.	189
Heaven is not given for our good works here	iii.	203
Hell is no other, but a soundlesse pit	iii.	173
Hell is the place where whipping-cheer abounds	iii.	173
Help me, *Julia,* for to pray	iii.	70

	Vol.	Page
Helpe me! helpe me! now I call	i.	17
Hence a blessed soule is fled	ii.	182
Hence, hence, profane; soft silence let us have	i.	154
Hence, hence prophane, and none appeare	iii.	162
Hence they have born my Lord; behold! the Stone	iii.	223
Her Eyes the Glow-worme lend thee	ii.	191
Her pretty feet	ii.	153
Here a little child I stand	iii.	158
Here a pretty Baby lies	ii.	203
Here a solemne Fast we keepe	ii.	113
Here down my wearyed limbs Ile lay	ii.	30
Here, here I live	ii.	116
Here, here I live with what my Board	ii.	164
Here I my selfe might likewise die	ii.	273
Here lies a Virgin, and as sweet	ii.	259
Here lyes *Johnson* with the rest	iii.	11
Here she lies, a pretty bud	ii.	32
Here she lyes (in Bed of Spice)	ii.	289
Here we are all, by day: By night w'are hurl'd	i.	35
Here we securely live, and eate	ii.	160
Herr. Come and let's in solemn wise	ii.	299
Hog has a place i'th' Kitchen, and his share	iii.	72
Holy-rood come forth and shield	ii.	126
Holy Water come and bring	ii.	262
Holy waters hither bring	iii.	36
Honour thy Parents; but good manners call	iii.	158
Honour to you who sit	ii.	266
Horne sells to others teeth; but has not one	ii.	183
How am I bound to Two! God, who doth give	iii.	144

	Vol.	Page
How am I ravisht! when I do but see	ii.	59
How can I choose but love, and follow her	ii.	133
How co'd *Luke Smeaton* weare a shoe, or boot	ii.	230
How dull and dead are books, that cannot show	ii.	62
How fierce was I, when I did see	iii.	20
How long, *Perenna*, wilt thou see	ii.	125
How Love came in, I do not know	i.	39
How rich a man is, all desire to know	ii.	42
How rich and pleasing thou, my *Julia* art	i.	50
How well contented in this private *Grange*	iii.	47
Humble we must be, if to Heaven we go	iii.	156
Huncks ha's no money (he do's sweare, or say)	ii.	119
Hye hence, pale Care, noe more remember	iii.	106

I.

	Vol.	Page
I abhor the slimie kisse	ii.	302
I a *Dirge* will pen for thee	iii.	37
I am holy, while I stand	ii.	208
I am of all bereft	ii.	119
I am Sive-like, and can hold	ii.	20
I am zeallesse; prethee pray	ii.	294
I askt my *Lucia* but a kisse	ii.	184
I ask't thee oft, what Poets thou hast read	i.	114
I beginne to waine in sight	ii.	131
I brake thy Bracelet 'gainst my will	ii.	230
I bring ye Love. *Quest.* What will love do?	iii.	46
I burn, I burn; and beg of you	i.	85
I call, I call: who doe ye call?	ii.	11
I can but name thee, and methinks I call	ii.	45
I cannot love, as I have lov'd before	ii.	261

	Vol.	Page
I cannot pipe as I was wont to do	ii.	172
I cannot suffer; and in this, my part	ii.	111
I co'd but see thee yesterday	ii.	285
I co'd never love indeed	ii.	134
I could wish you all, who love	ii.	22
I crawle, I creep; my *Christ*, I come	iii.	182
I dare not ask a kisse	ii.	215
I dislikt but even now	ii.	87
I do believe, that die I must	iii.	150
I do not love, nor can it be	ii.	87
I do not love to wed	ii.	96
I doe love I know not what	ii.	179
I dream'd this mortal part of mine	i.	28
I dream'd we both were in a bed	i.	34
I dreamt, last night, Thou didst transfuse	iii.	148
I dreamt the Roses one time went	i.	13
I feare no Earthly Powers	i.	111
I feeze, I freeze, and nothing dwels	i.	14
I have a leaden, thou a shaft of gold	iii.	84
I have been wanton, and too bold I feare	iii.	78
I haue behelde two louers, in a night	iii.	101
I have lost, and lately, these	i.	27
I have my Laurel Chaplet on my head	iii.	66
I have seen many Maidens to have haire	ii.	172
I heard ye co'd coole heat; and came	ii.	90
I held Love's head while it did ake	ii.	144
I lately fri'd, but now behold	iii.	13
I make no haste to have my Numbers read	ii.	193
I must	iii.	43
I plaid with Love, as with the fire	ii.	169

	Vol.	Page
I prest my *Julia's* lips, and in the kisse	ii.	230
I saw about her spotlesse wrist	i.	110
I saw a Cherry weep, and why?	i.	19
I saw a Flie within a Beade	ii.	280
I send, I send here my supremest kiss	iii.	56
I sing of *Brooks*, of *Blossomes*, Birds, and Bowers	i.	7
I sing thy praise *Iacchus*	ii.	263
I've paid Thee, what I promis'd; that's not All	ii.	110
I who have favour'd many, come to be	ii.	65
I will be short, and having quickly hurl'd	iii.	27
I will confesse	iii.	23
I will no longer kiss	iii.	77
I would to God, that mine old age might have	iii.	172
If Accusation onely can draw blood	ii.	155
If after rude and boystrous seas	i.	164
If all transgressions here should have their pay	iii.	126
If any thing delight me for to print	iii.	144
If, deare *Anthea*, my hard fate it be	i.	19
If felt and heard, (unseen) thou dost me please	iii.	82
If hap it must, that I must see thee lye	iii.	29
If I dare write to You, my Lord, who are	ii.	143
If I have plaid the *Truant*, or have here	iii.	215
If I kisse *Anthea's* brest	i.	102
If I lye unburied Sir	ii.	282
If Kings and kingdomes, once distracted be	iii.	81
If little labour, little are our gaines	ii.	254
If meat the Gods give, I the steame	i.	37
If men can say that beauty dyes	ii.	169
If 'mongst my many Poems, I can see	i.	108

	Vol.	Page
If Nature do deny	ii.	203
If nine times you your Bride-groome kisse	ii.	178
If so be a Toad be laid	ii.	180
If that my Fate has now fulfill'd my yeere	ii.	295
If thou aske me (Deare) wherefore	ii.	141
If Thou beest taken, *God* forbid	iii.	218
If thou dislik'st the Piece thou light'st on first	i.	11
If thou hast found an honie-combe	iii.	11
If warre, or want shall make me grow so poore	iii.	131
If well the Dice runne, lets applaud the cast	ii.	193
If well thou hast begun, goe on fore-right	ii.	32
If when these Lyricks (CESAR) You shall heare	ii.	4
If wholsome Diet can re-cure a man	iii.	62
If wounds in clothes, *Cuts* calls his rags, 'tis cleere	ii.	68
If ye feare to be affrighted	iii.	68
If ye will with *Mab* find grace	ii.	165
I'le come, I'le creep, (though Thou dost threat)	iii.	135
Ile come to thee in all those shapes	i.	100
I'le do my best to win, when'ere I wooe	i.	51
Ile get me hence	ii.	186
I'le hope no more	iii.	166
Ile sing no more, nor will I longer write	ii.	210
Ile to thee a Simnell bring	ii.	224
Ile write, because Ile give	i.	54
Il'e write no more of Love; but now repent	iii.	86
I'm free from thee; and thou no more shalt heare	i.	29
I'm sick of Love; O let me lie	ii.	92
Immortall clothing I put on	ii.	281

	Vol.	Page
Imparitie doth ever discord bring	ii.	279
In a Dreame, Love bad me go.	ii.	195
In all our high designments, 'twill appeare	iii.	17
In all thy need, be thou possest.	ii.	242
In Battailes what disasters fall	iii.	13
In Den'-shire Kerzie *Lusk* (when he was dead).	iii.	83
In desp'rate cases, all, or most are known.	ii.	284
In doing justice, God shall then be known	iii.	209
In God there's nothing, but 'tis known to be	iii.	189
In Gods commands, ne're ask the reason why	iii.	215
In holy meetings, there a man may be	ii.	101
In man, Ambition is the common'st thing.	i.	35
In Numbers, and but these few.	iii.	128
In Prayer the Lips ne're act the winning part	iii.	129
In sober mornings, doe not thou reherse	i.	11
In the hope of ease to come	iii.	56
In the houre of my distresse	iii.	132
In the morning when ye rise	iii.	67
In the old Scripture I have often read	iii.	129
In things a moderation keepe	ii.	267
In this little Urne is laid	ii.	268
In this little Vault she lyes	i.	87
In this misfortune Kings doe most excell	iii.	18
In this world (the *Isle of Dreames*)	iii.	180
In time of life, I grac't ye with my Verse	ii.	57
In vain our labours are, whatsoe're they be	iii.	184
In wayes to greatnesse, think on this	ii.	211
In's *Tusc'lanes*, *Tullie* doth confesse	iii.	83
Instead of Orient Pearls, of Jet	i.	23
Instruct me now, what love will do	iii.	71

	Vol.	Page
Is this a Fast, to keep	iii.	204
Is this a life, to break thy sleep	ii.	218
Is *Zelot* pure? he is: ye see he weares	ii.	217
It is sufficient if we pray	i.	101
It was, and still my care is	ii.	221

J.

	Vol.	Page
Jacob Gods Beggar was; and so we wait	iii.	190
Jealous Girles these sometimes were	ii.	142
Jehovah, as *Boëtius* saith	iii.	190
Jone is a wench that's painted	ii.	211
Jone wo'd go tel her haires; and well she might	ii.	155
Jolly and *Jillie*, bite and scratch all day	ii.	88
Jove may afford us thousands of reliefs	ii.	84
Judith has cast her old-skin, and got new	ii.	62
Julia and I did lately sit	i.	32
Julia, I bring	i.	112
Julia, if I chance to die	i.	35
Jvlia was carelesse, and withall	i.	21
Julia, when thy *Herrick* dies	ii.	141
Justly our *dearest Saviour* may abhorre us	iii.	200

K.

	Vol.	Page
Kindle the Christmas Brand and then	iii.	5
Kings must be dauntlesse: Subjects will contemne	iii.	79
Kings must not oft be seen by publike eyes	ii.	224
Kings must not only cherish up the good	ii.	266
Kings must not use the Axe for each offence	iii.	46
Kissing and bussing differ both in this	ii.	145

	Vol.	Page
Knew'st thou, one moneth wo'd take thy life away	ii.	232
Know when to speake; for many times it brings	iii.	60

L.

	Vol.	Page
Labour we must, and labour hard	iii.	186
Lacon. For a kiss or two, confesse	iii.	39
Laid out for dead, let thy last kindnesse be	i.	32
Lasciviousnesse is known to be	iii.	184
Last night I drew up mine Account	iii.	168
Last night thou didst invite me home to eate	ii.	97
Lay by the good a while; a resting field	iii.	16
Learn this of me, where e'r thy Lot doth fall	ii.	83
Leech boasts, he has a Pill, that can alone	ii.	34
Let all chaste Matrons, when they chance to see	i.	100
Let but thy voice engender with the string	i.	178
Let faire or foule my Mistresse be	ii.	177
Let Kings and Rulers learne this line from me	iii.	34
Let Kings Command, and doe the best they may	ii.	58
Let me be warme; let me be fully fed	i.	52
Let me not live, if I not love	iii.	74
Let me sleep this night away	ii.	163
Let moderation on thy passions waite	iii.	60
Let not that Day Gods Friends and Servants scare	iii.	180
Let not thy Tomb-stone er'e be laid by me	ii.	301
Let others looke for Pearle and Gold	iii.	144
Let others to the Printing Presse run fast	iii.	53
Let there be Patrons; Patrons like to thee	i.	70
Let the superstitious wife	iii.	3

	Vol.	Page
Let us now take time, and play . . .	ii.	227
Let us (though late) at last (my *Silvia*) wed	i.	13
Let's be jocund while we may . . .	ii.	203
Lets call for *Hymen* if agreed thou art	ii.	267
Let's live in hast; use pleasures while we may	ii.	115
Let's live with that smal pittance that we have	ii.	186
Lets now take our time	ii.	277
Let's strive to be the best; the Gods, we know it	iii.	46
Letcher was Carted first about the streets	ii.	155
Life is the Bodies light; which once declining	ii.	176
Life of my life, take not so soone Thy flight	i.	125
Like those infernall Deities which eate	ii.	284
Like to a Bride, come forth, my Booke, at last	i.	131
Like to the Income must be our expence	ii.	22
Like will to like, each Creature loves his kinde	iii.	61
Lillies will languish; Violets look ill .	i.	70
Linnit playes rarely on the Lute, we know	ii.	78
Little you are; for Womans sake be proud	ii.	184
Live by thy Muse thou shalt; when others die	ii.	182
Live, live with me, and thou shalt see	ii.	150
Live with a thrifty, not a needy Fate .	i.	21
Long Locks of late our Zelot *Peason* weares	ii.	290
Looke in my Book, and herein see .	iii.	9
Look how our foule Dayes do exceed our faire	iii.	119
Look, how the *Rainbow* doth appear	ii.	60
Look upon *Sapho's* lip, and you will swear	iii.	41
Lord, do not beat me	iii.	138
Lord, I am like to *Misletoe* . . .	iii.	171
Lord, I confesse, that Thou alone art able	iii.	148

	Vol.	Page
Lord, Thou hast given me a cell	iii.	135
Lost to the world ; lost to my selfe ; alone	iii.	26
Loth to depart, but yet at last, each one	ii.	61
Love and my selfe (beleeve me) on a day	i.	29
Love and the *Graces* evermore do wait	ii.	256
Love bade me aske a gift	i.	174
Love brought me to a silent Grove	ii.	296
Love he that will; it best likes me	ii.	88
Love, I have broke	ii.	117
Love, I recant	i.	173
Love in a showre of Blossomes came	iii.	1
Love is a Circle, and an Endlesse Sphere	ii.	289
Love is a circle that doth restlesse move	i.	21
Love is a kind of warre: Hence those who feare	ii.	300
Love is a Leven, and a loving kisse	iii.	26
Love is a sirrup; and who er'e we see	iii.	25
Love is maintain'd by wealth; when all is spent	ii.	222
Love, like a Beggar, came to me	iii.	21
Love, like a Gypsie, lately came	i.	108
Love love begets; then never be	ii.	251
Love, love me now, because I place	ii.	295
Love on a day (wise Poets tell)	ii.	2
Love scorch'd my finger, but did spare	i.	47
Love's a thing, (as I do heare)	ii.	21
Love-sick I am, and must endure	i.	103
Love's of it self, too sweet; the best of all	iii.	75
Luggs by the Condemnation of the Bench	i.	138
Lulls swears he is all heart; but you'l suppose	iii.	2
Lungs (as some say) ne'r sets him down to eate	ii.	201
Lupes for the outside of his suite has paide	iii.	34

M.

	Vol.	Page
Magot frequents those houses of good-cheere	ii.	149
Maidens tell me I am old	ii.	293
Maids nay's are nothing, they are shie	ii.	247
Make haste away, and let one be	ii.	290
Make, make me Thine, my gracious God	iii.	138
Make me a heaven; and make me there	i.	81
Man is a Watch, wound up at first, but never	ii.	167
Man is compos'd here of a two-fold part	ii.	83
Man knowes where first he ships himselfe; but he	ii.	125
Man may at first transgress, but next do well	iii.	53
Man may want Land to live in; but for all	ii.	278
Man must do well out of a good intent	iii.	14
Mans disposition is for to requite	iii.	17
Many we are, and yet but few possesse	ii.	125
May his pretty Duke-ship grow	ii.	5
Me thought I saw (as I did dreame in bed)	iii.	52
Me thought (last night) Love in an anger came	i.	27
Mease brags of Pullets which he eats: but Mease	ii.	64
Megg yesterday was troubled with a Pose	iii.	23
Men are not born Kings, but are men renown'd	ii.	231
Men are suspicious; prone to discontent	iii.	16
Men must have Bounds how farre to walke; for we	iii.	42
Men say y'are faire; and faire ye are, 'tis true	i.	171
Mercy, the wise Athenians held to be	iii.	186
Mighty *Neptune*, may it please	ii.	41
Milk stil your Fountains, and your Springs, for why?	ii.	286

	Vol.	Page
Mine eyes, like clouds, were drizling raine	ii.	226
Mon. Bad are the times. *Sil.* And wors then they are we.	ii.	93
Mony thou ow'st me; Prethee fix a day	i.	144
Moon is an Usurer, whose gain	ii.	66
Mop-ey'd I am, as some have said	i.	170
More discontents I never had	i.	32
More white then whitest Lillies far	i.	57
Much-more, provides, and hoords up like an Ant	i.	127
Mudge every morning to the Postern comes	iii.	32
Musick, thou *Queen of Heaven*, Care-charming spel	i.	179
My dearest Love, since thou wilt go	iii.	69
My faithful friend, if you can see	i.	137
My God, I'm wounded by my sin	iii.	124
My God! looke on me with Thine eye	iii.	126
My head doth ake	ii.	181
My *Lucia* in the deaw did go	ii.	243
My many cares and much distress	iii.	51
My Muse in Meads has spent her many houres	i.	163
My soule would one day goe and seeke	ii.	301
My wearied Barke, O let it now be Crown'd!	iii.	87
My wooing's ended: now my weddings neere	ii.	131

N.

	Vol.	Page
Naught are all Women; I say no	iii.	2
Need is no vice at all; though here it be	ii.	229
Nero commanded; but withdrew his eyes	ii.	223
Never my Book's perfection did appeare	i.	173
Never was Day so over-sick with showres	i.	88

	Vol.	Page
Next is your lot (Faire) to be number'd one	ii.	145
Night hath no wings, to him that cannot sleep	iii.	149
Night hides our thefts; all faults then pardon'd be	ii.	180
Night makes no difference 'twixt the Priest and Clark	ii.	297
Nis, he makes Verses; but the Lines he writes	iii.	6
No fault in women to refuse	ii.	23
No grief is grown so desperate, but the ill	iii.	62
No man comes late unto that place from whence	ii.	210
No man is tempted so, but may o'recome	iii.	201
No man so well a Kingdome Rules, as He	iii.	71
No man such rare parts hath, that he can swim	iii.	26
No more my *Silvia*, do I mean to pray	ii.	172
No more shall I, since I am driven hence	ii.	46
No news of Navies burnt at Seas	ii.	36
No question but *Dols* cheeks wo'd soon rost dry	iii.	72
No trust to Metals nor to Marbles, when	iii.	113
No wrath of Men, or rage of Seas	ii.	188
Noah the first was (as Tradition sayes)	iii.	197
None goes to warfare, but with this intent	i.	71
Noone-day and Midnight shall at once be seene	i.	101
Nor is my Number full, till I inscribe	ii.	162
Nor art thou lesse esteem'd, that I have plac'd	ii.	258
Nor thinke that Thou in this my Booke art worst	iii.	77
Not all thy flushing Sunnes are set	i.	124
Nothing can be more loathsome, then to see	ii.	184
Nothing comes Free-cost here; *Jove* will not let	ii.	125
Nothing hard, or harsh can prove	ii.	230
Nothing is New; we walk where others went	ii.	60

FIRST LINES.

	Vol.	Page
Now, if you love me, tell me	iii.	64
Now is the time for mirth	i.	138
Now is the time, when all the lights wax dim	i.	34
Now is your turn, (my Dearest) to be set	ii.	272
Now, now the mirth comes	iii.	58
Now, now's the time; so oft by truth	i.	90
Now *Patrick* with his footmanship has done	ii.	92
Now thou art dead, no eye shall ever see	iii.	33

O.

	Vol.	Page
O Earth! Earth! Earth! heare thou my voice, and be	i.	33
O Jealousie, that art	ii.	114
O *Jupiter*, sho'd I speake ill	ii.	248
O Thou, the wonder of all dayes!	iii.	151
O! Times most bad	ii.	183
O Yeares! and Age! Farewell	iii.	142
O! you the Virgins nine!	ii.	210
Of all our parts, the eyes expresse	ii.	28
Of all the good things whatsoe're we do	iii.	224
Of all those three-brave-brothers, faln i' th' Warre	ii.	113
Of both our Fortunes good and bad we find	ii.	260
Of Flanks and Chines of Beefe doth *Gorrell* boast	i.	155
Of fourre teeth onely *Bridget* was possest	ii.	92
Of Pushes *Spalt* has such a knottie race	ii.	182
Offer thy gift; but first the Law commands	iii.	28
Oft bend the Bow, and thou with ease shalt do	ii.	239
Oft have I heard both Youths and Virgins say	ii.	77
Old Parson *Beanes* hunts six dayes of the week	ii.	101

	Vol.	Page
Old Widdow *Prouse* to do her neigbbours evill	ii.	275
Old Widow *Shopter*, whensoere she cryes	iii.	82
Old wives have often told, how they	i.	30
On, as thou hast begunne, brave youth, and get	ii.	79
On with thy worke, though thou beest hardly prest	iii.	49
Once on a Lord-Mayors day, in Cheapside, when	ii.	163
One ask'd me where the roses grew?	i.	30
One Birth our Saviour had; the like none yet	iii.	193
One Eare tingles; some there be	iii.	79
One feeds on Lard, and yet is leane	ii.	119
One man repentant is of more esteem	iii.	199
One more by Thee, Love, and Desert have sent	ii.	148
One night i' th' yeare, my dearest Beauties, come	ii.	200
One of the five straight branches of my hand	ii	170
One onely fire has Hell; but yet it shall	iii.	204
One silent night of late	i.	43
One silver spoon shines in the house of *Croot*	iii.	82
Onely a little more	i.	146
Open thy gates	iii.	170
Or lookt I back unto the Times hence flown	ii.	220
Orpheus he went (as Poets tell)	ii.	274
Other mens sins wee ever beare in mind	ii.	253
Our Bastard-children are but like to Plate	iii.	51
Our Crosses are no other then the rods	ii.	296
Our Honours, and our Commendations be	ii.	27
Our *Houshold-gods* our Parents be	ii.	207
Our mortall parts may wrapt in Seare-cloths lye	ii.	163

	Vol.	Page
Our present Teares here (not our present laughter)	iii.	157
Out of the world he must, who once comes in	ii.	163

P.

	Vol.	Page
Pagget, a School-boy, got a Sword, and then	i.	111
Paradise is (as from the Learn'd I gather)	iii.	191
Pardon me God, (once more I Thee intreat)	iii.	171
Pardon my trespasse (Silvia,) I confesse	iii.	19
Parrat protests 'tis he, and only he	ii.	141
Partly worke and partly play	iii.	55
Part of the worke remaines; one part is past	iii.	87
Paske, though his debt be due upon the day	ii.	64
Paul, he began ill, but he ended well	iii.	198
Pauls hands do give; what give they, bread or meat	ii.	245
Peapes he do's strut, and pick his Teeth, as if	ii.	287
Permit me, *Julia*, now to goe away	i.	102
Permit mine eyes to see	iii.	168
Ph. Charon! O gentle *Charon!* let me wooe thee	ii.	244
Phœbus! when that I a Verse	ii.	29
Pievish doth boast, that he's the very first	ii.	88
Physitians say Repletion springs	iii.	26
Physitians fight not against men; but these	ii.	207
Play I co'd once; but (gentle friend) you see	i.	146
Play, *Phœbus* on thy Lute	ii.	81
Play their offensive and defensive parts	iii.	170
Please your Grace, from out your Store	ii.	202
Ponder my words, if so that any be	iii.	13

	Vol.	Page
Praise they that will Times past, I joy to see	iii.	18
Prat he writes Satyres; but herein's the fault	ii.	227
Prayers and Praises are those spotlesse two	iii.	122
Predestination is the Cause alone	iii.	202
Prepare for Songs; He's come, He's come	iii.	161
Preposterous is that Government, (and rude)	ii.	157
Prepost'rous is that order, when we run	ii.	232
Prickles is waspish, and puts forth his sting	iii.	9
Prig now drinks Water, who before drank Beere	i.	123
Prigg, when he comes to houses, oft doth use	ii.	66
Princes and Fav'rites are most deere, while they	ii.	256
Prue, my dearest Maid, is sick	ii.	29
Pusse and her Prentice both at Draw-gloves play	ii.	265
Put off Thy Robe of *Purple*; then go on	iii.	216
Put on thy *Holy Fillitings*, and so	iii.	7
Put on your silks; and piece by piece	i.	33
Putrefaction is the end	ii.	100

R.

	Vol.	Page
Ralph pares his nayles, his warts, his cornes, and *Ralph*	iii.	29
Rapine has yet tooke nought from me	iii.	179
Rare are thy cheeks *Susanna*, which do show	ii.	153
Rare is the voice itselfe; but when we sing	iii.	81
Rare Temples thou hast seen, I know	i.	156
Raspe playes at Nine-holes; and 'tis known he gets	ii.	84
Reach, with your whiter hands, to me	ii.	139

	Vol.	Page
Read thou my Lines, my *Swetnaham*, if there be	iii.	76
Readers, wee entreat ye pray	ii.	279
Reape's eyes so rawe are, that (it seemes) the flyes	ii.	303
Reproach we may the living; not the dead	ii.	194
Rise, Houshold-gods, and let us goe	ii.	10
Roaring is nothing but a weeping part	iii.	187
Rook he sells feathers, yet he still doth crie	ii.	102
Roots had no money; yet he went o'th score	ii.	99
Roses at first were white	ii.	1
Roses, you can never die	iii.	70
Rumpe is a Turne-broach, yet he seldome can	iii.	82
Rush saves his shooes, in wet and snowie wether	iii.	84

S.

	Vol.	Page
Sabbaths are threefold, as S. *Austine* sayes	iii.	197
Sadly I walk't within the field	i.	126
Sapho, I will chuse to go	ii.	276
Science in God, is known to be	iii.	183
Science puffs up, sayes *Gut*, when either Pease.	iii.	75
Scobble for Whoredome whips his wife; and cryes	i.	75
Sea-born Goddesse, let me be	ii.	58
Seeal'd up with Night-gum, Loach each morning lyes	ii.	280
See, and not see; and if thou chance t'espie	i.	53
See how the poore do waiting stand	ii.	59
Seeing thee *Soame*, I see a Goodly man	ii.	124
See'st thou that Cloud as silver cleare	ii.	59
Seest thou that Cloud that rides in State	ii.	280

	Vol.	Page
Seest thou those *Diamonds* which she weares	ii.	44
Shall I a daily Begger be	iii.	51
Shall I go to Love and tell	ii.	287
Shame checks our first attempts; but then 'tis prov'd	iii.	156
Shame is a bad attendant to a State	ii.	133
Shapcot! to thee the Fairy State.	ii.	24
Shark when he goes to any publick feast	ii.	24
She by the River sate, and sitting there	ii.	250
She wept upon her cheeks, and weeping so	ii.	250
Shew me thy feet; shew me thy legs, thy thighes	ii.	85
Shift now has cast his clothes; got all things new	ii.	68
Sho'd I not put on Blacks, when each one here	iii.	10
Shut not so soon; the dull-ey'd night	ii.	102
Sibb when she saw her face how hard it was	ii.	246
Sick is *Anthea*, sickly is the spring	iii.	64
Sin is an act so free, that if we shall	iii.	202
Sin is the cause of death; and sin's alone	iii.	203
Sin leads the way, but as it goes, it feels	iii.	156
Sin never slew a soule, unlesse there went	iii.	202
Sin no existence: Nature none it hath	iii.	191
Sin once reacht up to Gods eternall Sphere	iii.	164
Since for thy full deserts (with all the rest)	ii.	82
Since *Gander* did his prettie Youngling wed	ii.	201
Since *Jack* and *Jill* both wicked be	ii.	101
Since shed or Cottage I have none	iii.	65
Since to th' Country first I came	ii.	134
Sing me to death; for till thy voice be cleare	ii.	81
Sinners confounded are a twofold way	iii.	201

	Vol.	Page
Sitting alone (as one forsook)	i.	86
Skinns he dined well to day; how do you think?	ii.	88
Skoles stinks so deadly, that his Breeches loath	ii.	207
Skrew lives by shifts; yet sweares by no small oathes	ii.	78
Skurffe by his Nine-bones sweares, and well he may	ii.	131
Slouch he packs up, and goes to sev'rall Faires.	ii.	254
Smooth was the Sea, and seem'd to call	iii.	20
Snare, ten i' th' hundred calls his wife; and why?	ii.	196
Sneape has a face so brittle, that it breaks	ii.	32
So Good-luck came, and on my roofe did light	i.	174
So long (it seem'd) as *Maries* Faith was small	iii.	196
So long you did not sing, or touch your Lute	i.	167
So look the mornings when the Sun	ii.	278
So looks *Anthea*, when in bed she lyes	i.	56
So smell those odours that do rise	ii.	69
So smooth, so sweet, so silv'ry is thy voice	i.	37
So soft streams meet, so springs with gladder smiles	i.	133
Some ask'd me where the *Rubies* grew?	i.	41
Some parts may perish; dye thou canst not all.	ii.	165
Some salve to every sore, we may apply	ii.	289
Some would know	i.	20
Sorrowes divided amongst many, lesse	ii.	229
Sorrowes our portion are: Ere hence we goe	iii.	151
Sound Teeth has *Lucie*, pure as Pearl, and small	ii.	207
Speak, did the Bloud of *Abel* cry	iii.	199
Spend Harmless shade, thy nightly Houres	iii.	12

	Vol.	Page
Spenke has a strong breath, yet short Prayers saith	iii.	1
Spokes, when he sees a rosted Pig, he swears	iii.	38
Spring with the Larke, most comely Bride, and meet	ii.	191
Spunge makes his boasts that he's the onely man	ii.	115
Spur jingles now, and sweares by no meane oathes	iii.	79
Stand by the *Magick* of my powerfull Rhymes	ii.	298
Stand forth, brave man, since fate has made thee here	ii.	250
Stand with thy Graces forth, Brave man, and rise	ii.	132
Stately Goddesse, do thou please	ii.	63
Stay while ye will, or goe	i.	144
Still take advice; though counsels, when they flye	iii.	60
Still to our gains our chief respect is had	ii.	60
Store of courage to me grant	ii.	80
Stripes justly given yerk us (with their fall)	iii.	63
Strut, once a Fore-man of a Shop we knew	i.	90
Studies themselves will languish and decay	iii.	58
Sudds Launders Bands in pisse; and starches them	i.	170
Suffer thy legs, but not thy tongue to walk	iii.	122
Suspicion, Discontent, and Strife	i.	84
Sweet *Amarillis*, by a Spring's	i.	79
Sweet are my *Julia's* lips and cleane	ii.	295
Sweet, be not proud of those two eyes	i.	105
Sweet *Bridget* blusht, & therewithall	ii.	169

FIRST LINES.

	Vol.	Page
Sweet Country life, to such unknown	ii.	212
Sweet *Oenone*, doe but say	ii.	272
Sweet virgin, that I do not set	ii.	70
Sweet Western Wind, whose luck it is	i.	179

T.

	Vol.	Page
Take mine advise, and go not neere	ii.	298
Tap (better known then trusted) as we heare	ii.	285
Teage has told lyes so long, that when *Teage* tells	ii.	303
Teares most prevaile; with teares too thou mayst move	iii.	8
Teares quickly drie: griefes will in time decay	iii.	18
Teares, though th'are here below the sinners brine	ii.	206
Tell, if thou canst (and truly) whence doth come	ii.	90
Tell me rich man, for what intent	iii.	210
Tell me, what needs those rich deceits	ii.	303
Tell me, young man, or did the Muses bring	iii.	27
Tell that Brave Man, fain thou wo'dst have access	iii.	31
Tell us, thou cleere and heavenly Tongue	iii.	165
Temptations hurt not, though they have accesse	iii.	151
Thanksgiving for a former, doth invite	iii.	134
Th'art hence removing, (like a Shepherds Tent)	ii.	144
Th'ast dar'd too farre; but Furie now forbeare	i.	142
That *Christ* did die, the *Pagan* saith	iii.	212
That flow of Gallants which approach	ii.	229
That for seven *Lusters* I did never come	i.	45
That Happines do's still the longest thrive	ii.	273

	Vol.	Page
That Houre-glasse, which there ye see	i.	75
That little prettie bleeding part	iii.	179
That Love last long; let it thy first care be	ii.	138
That love 'twixt men do's ever longest last	iii.	74
That Manna, which God on His people cast	iii.	185
That Morne which saw me made a Bride	ii.	8
That Prince must govern with a gentle hand	iii.	68
That Prince takes soone enough the Victors roome	ii.	7
That Prince, who may doe nothing but what's just	iii.	81
That Princes may possesse a surer seat	ii.	101
That there's a God, we all do know	iii.	209
That was the Proverb. Let my mistresse be	ii.	62
The Bad among the Good are here mixt ever	iii.	191
The bloud of *Abel* was a thing	iii.	199
The Body is the Soules poore house, or home	ii.	297
The body's salt, the soule is; which when gon	iii.	83
The bound (almost) now of my book I see	iii.	53
The Doctors, in the Talmud, say	iii.	200
The Eggs of Pheasants wrie-nosed *Tooly* sells	ii.	171
The factions of the great ones call	ii.	302
The fire of Hell this strange condition hath	iii.	199
The Gods require the thighes	ii.	247
The Gods to Kings the Judgement give to sway	ii.	8
The Hag is astride	ii.	205
The *Jewes* their beds, and offices of ease	iii.	196
The Jewes, when they built Houses (I have read)	iii.	192
The lesse our sorrowes here and suffrings cease	iii.	173
The *Lictors* bundl'd up their rods: beside	iii.	16
The longer thred of life we spin	iii.	185

FIRST LINES. 267

	Vol.	Page
The May-pole is up	ii.	228
The mellow touch of musick most doth wound	i.	20
The Mountains of the Scriptures are (some say)	iii.	187
The only comfort of my life	iii.	64
The Person crowns the Place; your lot doth fall	iii.	37
The Power of Princes rests in the Consent	iii.	71
The readinesse of doing, doth expresse	ii.	291
The repetition of the name made known	iii.	191
The Rose was sick, and smiling di'd	ii.	225
The Saints-bell calls; and, *Julia*, I must read.	ii.	179
The same, who crownes the Conquerour, will be	iii.	189
The seeds of *Treason* choake up as they spring.	i.	16
The shame of mans face is no more	iii.	190
The staffe is now greas'd	iii.	85
The strength of *Baptisme*, that's within	iii.	213
The sup'rabundance of my store	iii.	180
The teares of Saints more sweet by farre	iii.	185
The time the Bridegroom stayes from hence	iii.	187
The Twi-light is no other thing (we say)	iii.	62
The *Virgin Marie* was (as I have read)	iii.	195
The Virgin-Mother stood at distance (there)	iii.	192
The work is done; now let my *Lawrell* be	iii.	216
The worke is done: young men and maidens, set	iii.	87
Then did I live when I did see	iii.	53
There is no evill that we do commit	iii.	197
There's no constraint to do amisse	iii.	204
These fresh beauties (we can prove)	i.	25
These Springs were Maidens once that lov'd	ii.	130
These *Summer-Birds* did with thy master stay	ii.	80

268 INDEX OF

	Vol.	Page
These temp'rall goods God (the most Wise) commends	iii.	198
Things are uncertain, and the more we get.	iii.	58
This Axiom I have often heard	ii.	220
This Crosse-Tree here	iii.	221
This Day is Yours, *Great* CHARLES! and in this War	ii.	283
This day my *Julia* thou must make	ii.	277
This Ile tell ye by the way	iii.	67
This is my comfort, when she's most unkind	iii.	66
This is the height of Justice, that to doe	ii.	188
This Lady's short, that Mistresse she is tall	ii.	101
This rule of manners I will teach my guests	iii.	48
This Stone can tell the storie of my life	iii.	37
Those ends in War the best contentment bring	iii.	57
Those Garments lasting evermore	iii.	207
Those ills that mortall men endure	ii.	83
Those possessions short-liv'd are	ii.	232
Those Saints, which God loves best	iii.	126
Those Tapers, which we set upon the grave	iii.	193
Thou art a plant sprung up to wither never	i.	171
Thou art to all lost love the best	ii.	3
Thou bidst me come away	iii.	140
Thou bidst me come; I cannot come; for why	iii.	140
Thou cam'st to cure me (Doctor) of my cold	i.	170
Thou gav'st me leave to kisse	ii.	64
Thou had'st the wreath before, now take the Tree	ii.	79
Thou hast made many Houses for the Dead	ii.	294
Thou hast promis'd, Lord, to be	iii.	131

	Vol.	Page
Thou know'st, my *Julia*, that it is thy turne	ii.	158
Thou mighty Lord and master of the Lyre	ii.	300
Thou sail'st with others in this *Argus* here	i.	39
Thou saist thou lov'st me *Sapho;* I say no	ii.	298
Thou say'st I'm dull; if edge-lesse so I be	iii.	74
Thou sayest Loves Dart	ii.	286
Thou say'st my lines are hard	ii.	58
Thou seest me *Lucia* this year droope	iii.	35
Thou sent'st to me a True-love-knot; but I	ii.	120
Thou shalt not All die; for while Love's fire shines	ii.	66
Thou, thou that bear'st the sway	ii.	300
Thou who wilt not love, doe this	i.	132
Thou writes in Prose, how sweet all Virgins be	ii.	276
Though a wise man all pressures can sustaine	i.	103
Though by well-warding many blowes w'ave past	ii.	226
Though Clock	ii.	240
Though Frankinsense the *Deities* require	iii.	21
Though from without no foes at all we feare	iii.	18
Though good things answer many good intents.	ii.	10
Though hourely comforts from the Gods we see.	ii.	10
Though I cannot give thee fires	ii.	41
Though long it be, yeeres may repay the debt	ii.	209
Though Thou beest all that *Active Love*	iii.	211
Thousands each day passe by, which wee	ii.	220
Three fatall Sisters wait upon each sin	iii.	122
Three lovely Sisters working were	i.	31
Thrice, and above, blest (my soules halfe) art thou	i.	57
Thrice happie Roses, so much grac't, to have	ii.	247

	Vol.	Page
Through all the night	iii.	141
Thus I	ii.	127
Thy Azure Robe, I did behold	i.	114
Thy former coming was to cure	iii.	214
Thy sooty *Godhead*, I desire	ii.	188
Till I shall come again, let this suffice	ii.	71
Time is the Bound of things, where e're we go	ii.	260
Time was upon	iii.	130
'Tis a known principle in War	ii.	23
Tis but a dog-like madnesse in bad Kings	iii.	18
'Tis Ev'ning, my Sweet	ii.	156
'Tis hard to finde God, but to comprehend	iii.	122
'Tis Heresie in others: In your face	ii.	131
'Tis liberty to serve one Lord; but he	iii.	2
Tis much among the filthy to be clean	iii.	61
'Tis never, or but seldome knowne	ii.	272
Tis no discomfort in the world to fall	iii.	62
Tis not a thousand Bullocks thies	i.	36
'Tis not ev'ry day, that I	ii.	234
'Tis not greatness they require	i.	37
'Tis not the food, but the content	ii.	32
'Tis not the Walls, or purple, that defends	ii.	237
'Tis said, as *Cupid danc't among*	ii.	231
'Tis still observ'd, that Fame ne're sings	ii.	239
'Tis still observ'd, those men most valiant are	iii.	45
'Tis the Chyrurgions praise, and height of Art	ii.	278
'Tis worse then barbarous cruelty to show	ii.	163
To all our wounds, here, whatsoe're they be	iii.	203
To a Love-Feast we both invited are.	iii.	145
To an old soare a long cure must goe on	iii.	50

FIRST LINES.

	Vol.	Page
To Bread and Water none is poore	i.	55
To cleanse his eyes, *Tom Brock* makes much adoe	ii.	9
To conquer'd men, some comfort 'tis to fall	i.	86
To fetch me Wine my *Lucia* went	ii.	142
To find that Tree of Life, whose Fruits did feed	i.	105
To gather Flowers *Sappha* went	ii.	249
To get thine ends, lay bashfulnesse aside	i.	14
To him, who longs unto his CHRIST to go	iii.	183
To his Book's end this last line he'd have plac't	iii.	88
To house the Hag, you must doe this	iii.	3
To joyn with them who here confer	iii.	223
To loose the button, is no lesse	ii.	232
To me my *Julia* lately sent	i.	22
To-morrow, *Julia*, I betimes must rise	i.	178
To mortall men great loads allotted be	ii.	234
To my revenge, and to her desp'rate feares	i.	151
To paint the fiend, *Pink* would the Devill see	ii.	8
To Print our Poems, the propulsive cause	ii.	111
To read my Booke the Virgin shie	i.	10
To safe-guard Man from wrongs, there nothing must	i.	115
To seek of God more then we well can find	iii.	147
To sup with thee thou didst me home invite	ii.	268
To this *white Temple* of my *Heroes*, here	ii.	139
To work a *wonder*, God would have her shown	iii.	193
Tom Blinks his Nose, is full of wheales, and these	ii.	287
Tom shifts the Trenchers; yet he never can	ii.	274
Touch but thy Lire (my *Harrie*) and I heare	ii.	293

	Vol.	Page
Trap, of a Player turn'd a Priest now is	iii.	72
Tread Sirs, as lightly as ye can	ii.	206
Trigg having turn'd his sute, he struts in state	ii.	230
True mirth resides not in the smiling skin	iii.	123
True rev'rence is (as *Cassiodore* doth prove)	iii.	185
True to your self, and sheets, you'l have me swear	ii.	55
Truggin a Footman was; but now, growne lame	ii.	304
Trust me Ladies, I will do	ii.	126
Truth by her own simplicity is known	iii.	78
Truth is best found out by the time, and eyes	iii.	9
Tumble me down, and I will sit	ii.	222
'Twas but a single *Rose*	i.	87
'Twas *Cesars* saying: *Kings no lesse Conquerors are*	ii.	284
'Twas not Lov's Dart	ii.	98
Twice has *Pudica* been a Bride, and led	ii.	130
Twilight, no other thing is, Poets say	ii.	295
Twixt Kings and Subjects ther's this mighty odds	i.	20
'Twixt Kings & Tyrants there's this difference known	ii.	296
Twixt Truth and Errour; there's this difference known	iii.	58
Two instruments belong unto our God	iii.	210
Two of a thousand things, are disallow'd	i.	16
Two parts of us successively command	ii.	55
Two things do make society to stand	ii.	291

	Vol.	Page

U.

	Vol.	Page
Umber was painting of a Lyon fierce	ii.	172
Under a Lawne, then skyes more cleare	i.	42
Unto *Pastillus* ranke *Gorgonius* came	iii.	68
Up with the Quintill, that the Rout	iii.	41
Upon her cheekes she wept, and from those showers	ii.	170
Urles had the Gout so, that he co'd not stand	ii.	177
Vrsley, she thinks those Velvet Patches grace	ii.	159

V.

	Vol.	Page
Vineger is no other I define	iii.	32
Virgins promis'd when I dy'd	i.	74
Virgins, time-past, known were these	i.	109

W.

	Vol.	Page
Want is a softer Wax, that takes thereon	iii.	9
Wanton Wenches doe not bring	iii.	79
Wantons we are; and though our words be such	ii.	194
Wash clean the Vessell, lest ye soure	iii.	64
Wash your hands, or else the fire	ii.	271
Wassaile the Trees, that they may beare	ii.	271
Wat ever men for Loyalty pretend	iii.	85
Water, water I desire	i.	35
Water, Water I espie	i.	106
We are Coheires with *Christ;* nor shall His own	iii.	212
We blame, nay, we despise her paines	ii.	298
We credit most our sight; one eye doth please.	iii.	9

	Vol.	Page
We merit all we suffer, and by far	iii.	209
We pray 'gainst Warre, yet we enjoy no Peace	ii.	273
We read how *Faunus*, he the shepheards *God*	iii.	41
We Trust not to the multitude in Warre	iii.	14
We two are last in Hell : what may we feare	i.	55
Weelcome! but yet no entrance, till we blesse	ii.	33
Weepe for the dead, for they have lost this light	iii.	26
Weigh me the Fire ; or canst thou find	iii.	120
Welcome, *Great Cesar*, welcome now you are	iii.	30
Welcome, Maids of Honour	i.	143
Welcome, most welcome to our Vowes and us	i.	41
Welcome to this my Colledge, and though late	iii.	39
Were I to give thee *Baptime*, I wo'd chuse	i.	47
Were there not a Matter known	ii.	100
What are our patches, tatters, raggs, and rents	iii.	34
What can I do in Poetry	ii.	46
What! can my *Kellam* drink his Sack	iii.	14
What Conscience, say, is it in thee	ii.	111
What Fate decreed, Time now ha's made us see	ii.	254
What God gives, and what we take	iii.	158
What here we hope for, we shall once inherit	iii.	156
What I fancy, I approve	i.	18
What is a Kisse? Why this, as some approve	ii.	193
What is't that wasts a Prince? example showes	iii.	82
What is the reason *Coone* so dully smels?	ii.	181
What made that mirth last night? the neighbours say	ii.	196
What need we marry Women, when	iii.	25
What needs complaints	iii.	54
What now we like, anon we disapprove	ii.	148

	Vol.	Page
What off-spring other men have got	ii.	223
What others have with cheapnesse seene, and ease	iii.	80
What sweeter musick can we bring	iii.	159
What though my Harp, and Violl be	iii.	155
What though the Heaven be lowring now	ii.	144
What though the sea be calme? Trust to the shore	i.	147
What times of sweetnesse this faire day fore-shows	i.	74
What was't that fell but now	i.	128
What will ye (my poor Orphans) do	ii.	194
What Wisdome, Learning, Wit, or Worth	i.	81
What's got by Justice is establisht sure	iii.	53
What's that we see from far? the spring of Day	ii.	12
Whatever comes, let's be content withall	iii.	141
Whatsoever thing I see	ii.	252
When a Daffadill I see	i.	64
When a man's Faith is frozen up, as dead	iii.	151
When after many Lusters thou shalt be	ii.	216
When age or Chance has made me blind	i.	54
When all Birds els do of their musick faile	ii.	242
When as *Leander* young was drown'd	i.	71
When *Chub* brings in his harvest, still he cries	iii.	75
When ere my heart, Love's warmth, but enter-taines	i.	68
When feare admits no hope of safety, then	iii.	84
When first I find those Numbers thou do'st write	iii.	32
When flowing garments I behold	iii.	50

	Vol.	Page
When I a ship see on the Seas	iii.	173
When I a Verse shall make	ii.	185
When I behold a Forrest spread	ii.	168
When I behold Thee, almost slain	iii.	220
When I consider (Dearest) thou dost stay	ii.	152
When I departed am, ring thou my knell	ii.	11
When I did goe from thee, I felt that smart	i.	72
When I goe Hence, ye *Closet-Gods*, I feare	ii.	208
When I love, (as some have told)	ii.	171
When I of *Villars* doe but heare the name	ii.	56
When I shall sin, pardon my trespasse here	iii.	164
When I through all my many Poems look	i.	165
When I thy Parts runne o're, I can't espie	i.	16
When I thy singing next shall heare	i.	38
Whenas in silks my *Julia* goes	ii.	267
When *Jill* complaines to *Jack* for want of meate	ii.	141
When *Julia* blushes, she do's show	ii.	27
When *Julia* chid, I stood as mute the while	i.	100
When Lawes full power have to sway, we see	ii.	186
When man is punisht, he is plaguèd still	iii.	170
When my date's done, and my gray age must die	i.	67
When my off'ring next I make	ii.	92
When once the sin has fully acted been	iii.	130
When once the Soule has lost her way	iii.	208
When one is past, another care we have	i.	31
When others gain much by the present cast	ii.	68
When out of bed my Love doth spring	ii.	86
When *Pimpes* feet sweat (as they do often use)	iii.	83

	Vol.	Page
When some shall say, Faire once my *Silvia* was	i.	36
When that day comes, whose evening sayes I'm gone	i.	24
When thou do'st play, and sweetly sing	ii.	64
When Thou wast taken, Lord, I oft have read	iii.	218
When times are troubled, then forbeare; but speak	iii.	71
When to a House I come, and see	iii.	48
When to thy Porch I come, and (ravisht) see	iii.	70
When we 'gainst Satan stoutly fight, the more	iii.	172
When well we speak, & nothing do that's good	iii.	214
When what is lov'd is Present, love doth spring	i.	22
When Winds and Seas do rage	iii.	174
When with the Virgin morning thou do'st rise	ii.	39
When words we want, Love teacheth to endite	ii.	291
Whenere I go, or what so ere befalls	ii.	280
Where God is merry, there write down thy fears	iii.	145
Where love begins, there dead thy first desire	ii.	300
Where others love, and praise my Verses; still	i.	113
Where Pleasures rule a Kingdome, never there	iii.	75
Wherever Nodes do's in the Summer come	ii.	282
Whether I was my selfe, or else did see	iii.	73
While Fates permit us, let's be merry	ii.	117
While leanest Beasts in Pastures feed	i.	133
While, *Lydia*, I was lov'd of thee	i.	120
While the milder Fates consent	i.	66
While thou didst keep thy *Candor* undefil'd	i.	10
White as *Zenobias* teeth, the which the Girles	ii.	249
White though ye be; yet, Lillies, know	i.	127
Whither dost thou whorry me	ii.	91

	Vol.	Page
Whither, *Mad-maiden*, wilt thou roame?	i.	8
Whither? Say, whither shall I fly	i.	68
Who after his transgression doth repent	ii.	278
Who begs to die for feare of humane need	ii.	294
Who formes a Godhead out of Gold or Stone	ii.	22
Who may do most, do's least; The bravest will	iii.	65
Who plants an Olive, but to eate the Oile?	iii.	66
Who, railing, drives the Lazar from his door	ii.	228
Who read'st this Book that I have writ	ii.	211
Who to the North, or South, doth set	ii.	100
Who violates the Customes, hurts the Health	iii.	61
Who will not honour Noble Numbers, when	ii.	272
Who with a little cannot be content	ii.	186
Who with thy leaves shall wipe (at need)	i.	10
Whom sho'd I feare to write to, if I can	i.	109
Whose head befringèd with be-scatterèd tresses	iii.	91
Why doe not all fresh maids appeare	i.	180
Why doe ye weep, sweet Babes? can Tears	i.	181
Why do'st thou wound, & break my heart	iii.	76
Why I tye about thy wrist	ii.	40
Why, Madam, will ye longer weep	ii.	146
Why sho'd we covet much, whenas we know	iii.	45
Why so slowly do you move	ii.	292
Why this Flower is now call'd so	i.	24
Why walkes *Nick Flimsey* like a Male-content?	ii.	97
Why wore th' Egyptians Jewells in the Eare?	iii.	130
Will ye heare, what I can say	ii.	57
Wilt thou my true Friend be?	ii.	173
With blamelesse carriage, I liv'd here	i.	69
With golden Censers, and with Incense, here	iii.	166

	Vol.	Page
With paste of Almonds, *Syb* her hands doth scoure	ii.	168
Wither'd with yeeres, and bed-rid *Mumma* lyes	i.	156
Wo'd I see Lawn, clear as the Heaven, and thin?	ii.	92
Wo'd I wooe, and wo'd I winne	iii.	6
Wo'd yee have fresh Cheese and Cream?	ii.	135
Wo'd ye oyle of Blossomes get?	ii.	238
Woe, woe to them, who (by a ball of strife)	i.	43
Women, although they ne're so goodly make it.	ii.	222
Words beget Anger; Anger brings forth blowes	iii.	8
Wrinkles no more are, or no lesse	ii.	66
Wrongs, if neglected, vanish in short time	ii.	266
Y'ave laught enough (sweet), vary now your Text	ii.	10
Ye have been fresh and green	ii.	9
Ye may simper, blush, and smile	i.	127
Yee pretty Huswives, wo'd ye know	ii.	103
Yee silent shades, whose each tree here	ii.	112
You are a Lord, an Earle, nay more, a Man	ii.	118
You are a *Tulip* seen to day	i.	152
You aske me what I doe, and how I live?	iii.	50
You have beheld a smiling *Rose*	i.	129
You may vow Ile not forgett	iii.	108
You say I love not, 'cause I doe not play	i.	25
You say, to me-wards your affection's strong	i.	87
You say y'are sweet; how sho'd we know.	ii.	12
You say y'are young; but when your Teeth are told	ii.	119
You say you'l kiss me, and I thanke you for it	ii.	180

	Vol.	Page
You say, you love me; that I thus must prove	ii.	35
You see this gentle streame, that glides	ii.	238
Young I was, but now am old	i.	29

GLOSSARIAL INDEX
AND
INDEX OF NAMES.

GLOSSARIAL INDEX.

As a rule, the references given will guide to explanations or illustrations of the word or thing in the place or places. A few additions are made in the Index itself *s. v.* Nouns and verbs and other forms are placed together; also words occasionally different though spelled alike, e. g. neat=oxen, and elegant, but in the places the meaning will in each case be found. An earnest effort has been made to include every word in any way noticeable.

A.

Abby-Lubbers, i. 161.
Aches, ii. 51.
Action, i. 76.
Adulce, ii. 218.
Affection, iii. 207.
Ale-dy'd, ii. 196.
Alma, iii. 145.
Altar, hallowed, ii. 77.
All, and some, i. 132.
All-filling, iii. 209.
Allay, ii. 180.
Amber, i. 37, ii. 67.
Amber-greece, i. 8, 33 : ii. 172.
And, i. 103: iii. 176.
Apostate, ii. 15.*
Aprill day, ii. 259: iii. 103.

* Cf. Shirley :—
"And can thy proud apostate eyes
Court her again, with hope t' entice
One gentle language, or a smile
Upon a renegade so vile."
(Poems by Dyce, p. 146.)

Arch-antiquary, ii. 65.
Arks=baskets, ii. 9.
Armilet, i. 31.
Artlesse, i. cclix: ii. 79: iii. 132.
ΑΡΧΗ, iii. 224.
Ash-heapes, ii. 37.
Aspects, ii. 261.
Asse, iii. 80.
Assertion, ii. 86.
Auspice, iii. 7.
Auspicate, iii. 30.

B.

Babies, i. 26: ii. 27: 43, 153.
Bælus eye, ii. 118.
Babyship, i. 149.
Band=bond, iii. 48.
Banes, i. 68.
Baptime, i. 47, 166: iii. 162.
Barbels, ii. 49.
Barly-Break, i. 55, 96.
Bashfulnesse, ii. 232.
Bastard, ii. 269.
Batch, iii. 67.
Batten, ii. 164.
Baucis, ii. 51.

Baud, iii. 48.
Baudery, candle, ii. 50.
Beads, i. 117.
Beadsman, iii. 35.
Beames, i. 12.
Beans, ii. 94.
Bed-man=grave-maker, ii. 294.
Bedabled, ii. 13, 89, 243.
Bedangling, iii. 22.
Beere, ii. 72.
Behung, i. 28: ii. 50, 110.
Bellman, ii. 28: iii. 102, 134, 174.†
Bent, i. 161: ii. 94, 223: iii. 5.
Benizon, ii. 239: iii. 36.
Bepearl'd, ii. 178.
Bepranckt, ii. 151.
Beshiver'd, iii. 120.
Bespangling, i. 116.
Bestroaking, ii. 37.
Bestrutted, ii. 25-6.
Bethwack, iii. 63.
Beucolicks, i. 9: ii. 235.
Bewash, iii. 55.
Bewearied, ii. 54.

---

† So too later Cleveland (1669 p. 3):—
"Hark how the sprightly Chanticlere
That Baron Tell clock of the night."

Bice, i. 65.
Bin, ii. 128, 246.
Bishop't i. 109.
Black-bore, iii. 85.
Blacks = mourning garments, iii. 10, 62, 87.
Blaze, ii. 20.
Blew-ruler, ii. 123.
Blithefull, ii. 209.
Blouze, ii. 264.
Blush-guiltinesse, ii. 288.
Bodies, ii. 91.
'Bove, i. 77.
Bonnet, ii. 89.
Bo-peep, ii. 153.
Bousing, ii. 159.
Box, ii. 183: iii. 4.
Bran, iii. 216.
Brand, iii. 5.
Brasse, i. 50.
Brave, i. 173.
Bridgeman, i. 65.
Briefs, i. 66.
Bristle, ii. 18.

Broke heart, ii. 26.
Bruckel'd, i. 159.
Brusle, ii. 18.
Buck, ii. 126-7.‡
Buckittings, i. 35.
Buckram, ii. 23, 167.
Bucksome, ii. 38.
Bulging, i. 39.
Burle, ii. 182.
Burling, i. 65.
Burr, ii. 205.
Bussing, ii. 145.
Button'd-staffe, ii. 71, 190.

C.

Calamus, iii. 177.
Calenture, iii. 214.
Call, ii. 11.
Canary, ii. 75 : iii. 63.
Candid, ii. 110, 159, iii. 7.
Candidate, ii. 2, 280.
Candour, i. 10 : ii. 249 : iii. 98, 181.*
Candle-light, ii. 107.

‡ "Send me to the conduit with the water-tankard: I'll beat linen bucks, or anything to redeem my negligence." (T. Heywood's 2nd Part of "If you know not me, &c. Act I. i. 1606). See Merry Wives of Windsor iii. 5.

* Cf Landor in our own day, thus :—
"Negligent as the blossoms of the field,
 Array'd in candour and simplicity." (Count Julian.)

Capring, iii. 45.
Carbage, iii. 34.
Carkanet, i. 23, 50: ii. 44, 118, 150, 217.
Carrionere, ii. 184.
Casques, i. 26.
Caule, ii. 108: iii. 154.
Cecubum, ii. 178.
Cedar, i. 77, 108, 155: iii. 110.
Cense, ii. 106.
Cens'd, iii. 163.
Ceremonies, iii. 4, 5, 38.
Cess, i. 55.
Ceston, ii. 106.
Chamlets, i. 81.
Chardges, iii. 104.
Charme, ii. 160.
Charmes, iii. 2, 3.
Cherrylets, iii. 92.
Cherrypit, i. 32.
Chesnuts, fired, ii. 38.
Chev'rell, i. 123.
Chine, ii. 52.
Chips, ii. 169.
Childish, iii. 99.
Chirring, ii. 25.
Chit, ii. 202.
Chives, i. 163: ii. 46, 221.
Christal, i. 129.
Chop-cherry, ii. 64.

Circular, ii. 50.
Circumbends, i. 159.
Circumcrost, ii. 208.
Circumcision, ii. 217.
Circumflankt, ii. 251.
Circumfused, i. 119.
Circummortal, i. 168: ii. 110.
Circumspacious, iii. 31.
Circumspangle, ii. 277.
Circumgyration, iii. 32.
Circumstants, i. 137.
Circumvolving, iii. 110.
Cirque, ii. 78.
Citterne, iii. 60.
Civil, ii. 162, 216.
Civilly, ii. 155.
Civility, i. 47, 154: ii. 168.
Cleanly-Watonnesse, i. 7.
Closet-gods, i. 24.
Coats, i. 8.
Cob-web, i. 13.
Cockall, i. 159.
Cockes, i. 59.
Cock-rood, ii. 215.
Cockring, ii. 63.
Codlins, i. 159.
Codled, ii. 15.
Codpiece, i. 162: ii. 24.
Columbine, ii. 190: iii. 154.
Comming, ii. 149.
Commutual, i. 121.

Companie, ii. 101.
Compartlement, ii. 208.
Compost, ii. 263.
Comply, ii. 108, 175 : iii. 195.
Compulsive, iii. 74.
Confer, iii. 223.
Congesting, ii. 238.†
Consonant, ii. 181.
Contemnes, ii. 231.
Continent, ii. 142, 249.
Convinces, i. 133 : iii. 103.
Coorse, ii. 25.
Coosning, ii. 211.
Cornish, i. 157.
Corrols, ii. 191.
Counter, ii. 106.
Counter-changed, ii. 176.
Counter-feit, ii. 281.
Coveting, iii. 223.
Cowle=cowl, iii. 63.
Crack, iii. 62.
Creame=froth, i. 14.
Creeking, ii. 240.
Crosse and pile, ii. 145.
Crosse-line, i. 109.
Cruells, iii. 128.
Cuckoes spittle, ii. 25.

Cull'd, iii. 52.
Cunctation, ii. 250 : iii. 16.
Cup-shot, iii. 52.
Cure, ii. 289.
Curious-comely, ii. 208.

D.

Dampish, ii. 126.
Dandillions, ii. 108.
Daphne=laurel, ii. 65.
Dardanum, i. 50.
Daring, iii. 169.
Dead, ii. 271.
Deaf, ii. 217.
Deale, i. 42, 118 : iii. 176, 178.‡
Decent, ii. 243.
Decurted, iii. 7.
Denounc'd, i. 78.
Dereliction, iii. 189.
Descrie, iii. 50.
Deservelesse=undeserving. i. 132.
Designments, iii. 17.
Determines, ii. 176.
Devote, i. 46.
Dew, i. 99.

† Instead of quotation intended for the Memorial-Introduction, I must content myself with reference to my edition of Southwell. s.v.

‡ here=a good deal, considerable : in I. 118=a goodly number.

Dew-laps, ii. 213.
Diaper, ii. 203 : iii. 145.
Dictator, i. 38.
Ding-thrift, ii. 97.
Disacquainted, iii. 142.
Disadorn'd, ii. 288.
Discease, iii. 57.
Discruciate, ii. 229.
Disparkling, ii. 14.
Disposeresse, ii. 235.
Dollies, i. 66.
D'on, iii. 35, 140.
Doome, iii. 150, 189.
Domiduca, i. 92.
Doxy, i. 66.
Dow, ii. 281 : iii. 67, 176.
Draw-gloves, i. 172 : ii. 189, 265.
Dreadfulnesse, iii. 174.
Dreg'd, ii. 67.
Drive, ii. 127.
Drosomell, ii. 137.
Dry-rosted, i. 156.
Ductile, ii. 199.

E.

Eare, i. 38.
Eares, ii. 290.
East, iii. 43.
Echo, ii. 95.
Effused, ii. 200.

Effusions, i. 39 : ii. 195 : iii. 43.
Egge, ii. 59.
Elixar, iii. 197.
Ennamel'd, ii. 4.
Encarv'd, ii. 112.
Enchac't, i. 156.
Enchasing, ii. 107.
Enchequered, ii. 106.
Enclarited, ii. 57.
Encolouring, ii. 44.
Enfreez'd, ii. 107.
Enspangle, ii. 148.
Enspher'd, ii. 283.
Enspire, i. 146.
Enspir'd, i. 141 : iii. 50.
Enstile, ii. 121.
Entend, ii. 100, 188.
Enterplac't, iii. 40.
Enterwove, i. 170.
Erres, ii. 50 : iii. 209.
Erring, i. 46, 114.
Errour, ii. 108 : iii. 58.
Essay, ii. 72.
Euphonie, iii. 24.
Eure, iii. 145.
Evill, i. 105.
Excathedrated, i. 110.
Excruciate, iii. 204.
Eye, iii. 152.

GLOSSARIAL INDEX.

F.

Factours, ii. 69.
Fan, i. 77.
Fairies, i. 177.
Farc't, iii. 48.
Farcing, ii. 169.
Fardell, ii. 253.
Farre-fetch, iii. 100.
Fat-fed, ii. 71.
Fatts, i. 177.
Feare, iii. 158.
Female, ii. 294.
Feel, ii. 94.
Fellon, ii. 131.
Fetuous, i. 160.
Fier-drakes, iii. 103.
Filcher, i. 121, 122.
Fil'de, ii. 61.
Filitings, i. 19.
Fild-full, iii. 123.
Fill-horse, i. 176.
Firstling, i. 25.
Flagonet, ii. 269.
Flax, ii. 109.

Flitches=buttocks, ii. 264.
Flock, ii. 94.
Float, ii. 247.
Flosculet, ii. 36.
Flux, iii. 217.
Fly-blow, ii. 201.
Footmanship, ii. 92.
Fond, ii. 244.
Fondling, i. 19.
For and, iii. 176.*
Fore-fend, ii. 95.
Fore-right, ii. 32.
Fore-sounds, ii. 38.
Forgetfull, iii. 100.
Forked-Fee, ii. 167.
Forme, ii. 145.
Forum, Holy, ii. 2.
Fother, iii. 55.
Four-square, iii. 17.
Four-leav'd grasse=shamrock, ii. 106.
Fox i' th' hole, ii. 37, 214.
Foxe-furre, ii. 218.†
Frantick, ii. 160.

* "The lyght of the body is the eye. Wherfore yf thyne eye be single, all thy body shal be ful of lyght. *But and yf* thyne eye be wycked, all thy body shalbe full of darknesse."—The Great Bible, (Cranmer's, 1541)), Matthew vi., 22-3.

Also the same in Edmund Becke's, printed by Day and Serres, 1540.

† See note in this Glossary under (sagge).

Fresh-quilted, i. 116.
Frie, i. 68, 85, 106 : ii. 87, 170 : iii. 13.
From, ii. 175.
Froth, ii. 81.
Frumentie, i. 177.
Fulfill, ii. 239 : iii. 39.
Ful-filling, i. 165.
Full-stop, ii. 195.
Furre, i. 78.
Furr'd, ii. 9.
Fuz-ball, ii. 25, 202.

G.

Gall'd, i. 89.
Gamesome, iii. 40.
Gelli-flours, i. 128.
Gemmal ring, i. 112.
Gemmes, ii. 204.
Gentle-licking, i. 166.
Gentlenes, ii. 16.
Gentle-heart, ii. 17.
Genius, i. 168 : ii. 268.
Giblets, ii. 72.
Give, ii. 245.
Glade, ii. 215.
Gleab, ii. 263.
Globe, of radiant fire, ii. 176.*

Gloves, ii. 245.
Glut, iii. 145.
Gospel-tree, i. 34.
Gotiere, i. 67.
Gotwit, ii. 74.
Granges, ii. 117, 240.
Green-gown, i. 118.
Greenie-Kalendar, ii. 112.
Great-blew-ruler, ii. 123.
Griefs, small, i. 26.
Griest, iii. 180.
Grutch, ii. 19.
Guest-rite, ii. 72.
Guild, i. 88.
Guilded, ii. 131.

H.

Haires, iii. 153.
Hair-less, ii. 59.
Halcions, i. 156.
Hap, iii. 218.
Handsell, iii. 143, 157.
Handsome-handed, ii. 137.
Hat, ii. 68.
Hatcht, i. 161 : iii. 101.
Hay in's horn, ii. 104.
Hearce-cloth, i. 180 : iii. 153.
Heraldic terms, iii. 21.
Heyes, ii. 151.

* The promised quotations were crushed out. See my Memorial-Introduction to Giles Fletcher in this Series.

Hede, iii. 103.
Hisped, ii. 167.
Hock-cart, i. 7, 176.
Hoe, iii. 42.
Holme, ii. 204.
Holy, Forum, ii. 2.
Holy Grist, i. 159.
Holy Rood, ii. 126.
Hope-seed, i. 88.
Hoods, ii. 290.
Hoofy, iii. 105.
House, iii. 3.
Huckson, ii. 202.
Hug'd, ii. 147.
Hung, ii. 107.
Huswives, ii. 199.
Huswiferie, ii. 198.
Husband, ii. 263.
Hypostatical, iii. 200.

I.

I = ay or aye, i. 133, 160: ii. 279, 288 : iii. 36, 38, 40, 97.
Idoll-canker, i. 157
Immensive, i. 139.
Importance, iii. 193.
Inapostate, iii. 81.
Inarculum, ii. 158.
Incannonicall, iii. 80.
Incantation, ii. 174.
Incarnation, ii. 59.
Inchristalled, ii. 75.
Incivility. iii. 48.
Income, ii. 199.
Inconfused, iii. 196.
Incurl'd, ii. 253.
Incurious, ii. 257.
Indecencie, i. 16.
Infanta, ii. 177.
Infortunitie, iii. 28.
Ingot, ii. 212.
Ingression, ii. 208.
Injewel'd, ii. 12.
Instant, ii. 38, 161.
Interlaid, ii. 106.
Intertalkt, ii. 3.
Intext, ii. 208.
Intitled, iii. 185.
Iris, i. 102.
Irruption, iii. 127.
Issue, ii. 156.
Itchlesse, ii. 251.

J.

Jet, ii. 269 : iii. 37, 178.
Jewes, iii. 192.
Jimmal, ii. 120.
John Sir, ii. 178.
Joy-sops, iii. 59.
Jocond, iii. 88.
Junkets, ii. 256.

Just, ii. 295.
Justments, i. 45.

K.

Karkanet, i. 23.
Kathern, ii. 278.
Kenn, iii. 139.
Kerzie, iii. 83.
Kidney-lipt, i. 107.
Kisse, iii. 104.
Kitling and kitlings, i. 138 : ii. 25, 54, 107.
Knap, ii. 40.
Knot, ii. 298.

L.

Lace, i. 23.
Lachrimæ, ii, 67.
Lake, i. 65.
Ladanum, ii, 133.
Lambs-wool, iii. 59.
Larr, i. 62 : ii. 41, 46, 53, 71, 83, 99, 269.
Lares, i. 24 : ii. 129, 221.
Larded, ii. 269.
Lations, i. 81.
Launders, i. 170.
Laureat, ii. 63.
Laurell, i. 11.
Lautitious, ii. 269.
Lawne, i. 13.
Least, i. 179.
Lends, ii. 16.
Lemster Ore, ii. 105.*
Lesse, of heart, i. 169.
Leavens, iii. 67.
Levell-Coyle, iii. 50, 215.
Leven, ii. 162 : iii. 26, 41.
Lictors, iii. 16.
Lie, ii. 126.
Like, iii. 61.
Lillie-center, ii. 102.
Lilly-wristed, ii. 212.
Lip-labour, iii. 129.
Lively-hood, ii. 82.
Lobster, lady of the, i. 162.
Logomachie, iii. 8.
Love-lies-bleeding, i. 22.
Loving-lucklesse, i. 25.

---

* "As for the Wooll in this County, [Herefordshire,] it is best known to the honour thereof by the name of *Lempster Ore*, being absolutely the finest in this County and indeed in all England."— Fuller's Worthies, p. 33.

Similarly we read of an arm of the Zuyder Zee, as follows :— "In many places a very rich alluvion, forming a most valuable manure, is found at the bottom of these shallows; hence the name of Mer d' Or, or golden sea, the inhabitants deriving a golden harvest of hay from its employment on these meadows." ("The Dead Cities of the Zuyder Zee," by Havard, p. 29 : 1875.)

Lullaby, i. 149.
Lusters, i. 45 : ii. 216.
Lustie-gellie, iii. 29.

M.

Maidenhead, i. 59.*
Maids, ii. 157, 247.
Maidens-blush, ii. 17, 269.
Maiden-haire, i. 31, 89.
Male, ii. 294.
Male-incense, iii. 155.
Man, ii. 118.
Manchet, ii. 128.
Mantle, ii. 269.
Mantle-tree, ii. 46.
Mare, shooe the, ii. 37.
Margarite, iii. 100.
Margents, ii. 173.
Marjoram, ii. 12.
Marmelet, ii. 208.
Maronian, ii. 220.
Masterdom, iii. 201.

Mashes, ii. 303.
Mask, ii. 244.
Mattens, i. 150 : iii. 70.
Maukin, i. 175.
Maund, ii. 268 : iii. 69.
Maundie, iii. 176.
Maying, i. 116.
Meane, iii. 21, 61.
Meddow-verse, ii. 62.
Mell, ii. 67.
Merited, i. 21,—an odd misprint for 'invited' in footnote.
Mew, ii. 68.
Mew'd, ii. 217.
Miching, ii. 241.
Mincing, iii. 178.
Mickle, ii. 202.
Mirk, iii. 148.
Monilesse, iii. 144.
Mop-ey'd, i. 170.

* Cf. Shirley :—
   "For him to whom your heart is tied
   Keep it still virgin, and a bride,
   That often as you go to bed
   You give or take a maidenhead."
                    (Poems by Dyce, p. 434.)
Or as in Rawlinson MS. :—
   "May your husbands' love renew
   Every day their marriage vow,
   And yourselves, as newly wed,
   Give each night a maidenhead."

Moonlesse, i. 44.
Moon-tann'd, ii. 108.
Morris-dance, ii. 257.
Mosse-like, ii. 106.
Mothering, ii. 224.
Mowes, ii. 129.
Much-more, i. 127.
Mummeries, ii. 214.
Mute, iii. 36.

N.

Narde, i. 125.
Nature, iii. 102.
Nay's. ii. 247.
Neat, i. 9, 59, 177 : ii. 204, 213 : iii. 13.
Neat-herds, ii. 235.
Neat-herdesse, ii. 236: iii. 39.
Nectarell, i. 33.
Neech, i. 157.
Nerv'lits, i. 28.
Neere, ii. 129.
Newt's, ii. 26.
Nine-bones, ii. 131.
Nine-holes, ii. 84.
Niplet, ii. 102.
Nits, i. 162.
Nockt, iii. 148.
Nominate, iii. 210.
Nose, i. 139.
Novitie, iii. 211.
Num'rous, ii. 105 : iii. 105.
Nutts, i. 97.

O.

Oathes and lyes, ii. 135.*
Oate, ii. 136, 172, 235, 237.
Ode, iii. 102.
Offring, iii. 213.
Oke, i. 43.
One, i. 111.
Onely, ii. 143.

---

* Hooke in his Amanda says—"I will not
——Wrack my fancie for a kisse;
Fool to your laughing *Ladyship*,
To get a smile, or touch your lip;
Protest with oathes high and mighty,
That your spittle is *aqua vitæ*.

Amongst the gallants swear and rant.
And of your kindnesse boast and vant;
Then drink diseases down, and wave
All thoughts of sicknesse or the graue."
Amanda, p. 60.

Once, iii. 156, 206.
Or, ii. 29, 66.
Ore-buyer, iii. 64.
Ore-renetted, i. 11.
Ore-wash't, ii. 295.
Orgies, i. 12.
Orts, ii, 202.
Osiers, iii. 128.
Out-during, iii. 88.
Out-red, i. 19.
Over-cool'd, ii. 181.
Over-fill, ii. 217.
Over-leaven, iii. 65.
Owl-ey'd, ii. 20.

P.

Packs, i. 103 : ii. 234.
Paddocks, iii. 159.
Painfull, i. 60 : ii. 198.
Pap, i. 138.
Palsie-struck, i. 146.
Panier, ii. 203.
Pannicles, ii. 234.
Pansies, i. 128.
Paragon, i. 18, 132 : iii. 151.
Parasceve, iii. 145.
Parcell-gilt, iii. 46.
Paranæticall, ii. 218.
Parly, i. 13.
Parson, i. 160.

Pean-gardens, ii. 220.
Pearly-purling, i. 91.
Pease, ii. 202.
Peeps = pips or spots on a card, ii. 106.
Peculiar, iii. 65.
Peltish, ii. 105.
Perking, i. 79.
Permanent, iii. 94.
Perpolite, iii. 32.
Pesant, iii. 207.
Peter-penny, ii. 257.
Phill. i. 180 : ii. 141.
Philomel, ii. 245.
Pickt, locks, i. 118.
Picks, ii. 106.
Pie, iii. 40.
Piggin, iii. 172.
Pipkin, iii, 172.
Pipkinnet, iii. 182.
Pikes, iii. 170.
Pile, crosse and, ii. 145.
Pill, i. 54, ii. 284.
Pimpleides, ii. 287.
Pinner, ii. 265.
Pitcher, i. 19.
Pith, ii. 20, 25, 53, 261.
Plackets, iii. 55.
Plat, i. 19.
Platonick, ii. 148.

Plaudite, i. 164.*
Poesies, iii. 69.
Poetresse, ii. 5.
Poise, iii. 123.
Points, ii. 16.
Poking-sticks, ii. 302.
Pomander, i. 22-3 : ii. 133.
Poore, ii. 180.
Postern-bribe, ii. 167.
Post and Paire, ii. 228.†
Posts, i. 95.

Pounc't, i. 114.
Prank, i. 176 : iii. 178.
Pre-compos'd, ii. 208.
Predestination, ii. 86.
Predicant, ii. 80.
Preportions, ii. 232.
President, ii. 60.
Pression, ii. 248.
Prevaricate, i. 137.
Priestresse, ii. 158.
Pricelesse, i. 36.

* Erasmus, in his Apophth. says of Augustus Cæsar:—
When he perceiued and feled his diyng houre to approche, he enquired of his familiares, beyng let into his chamber to come and see him, whether it semed to them, that he had any thing handsomely enough played his parte in passyng his life.

"Meanyng of the trade and course of his presente life, which many writers doen resemble and compare vnto plaiyng a parte in an Enterlude. And then pronounced he this Greke verse folowing, customablie vsed to be soungen at the last end of Comedies, exhibited, and plaied to an ende.

$$\delta\acute{o}\tau\epsilon\ \kappa\rho\acute{o}\tau o\nu\ \kappa a\grave{\iota}\ \pi\acute{a}\nu\tau\epsilon\varsigma\ \dot{\eta}\mu\hat{\iota}\nu\ \mu\epsilon\tau\grave{a}\ \chi a\rho\hat{a}\varsigma\ \kappa\tau\upsilon\pi\acute{\eta}\sigma a\tau\epsilon.$$
"That is,
"Clappe hands, in signe of contentacion,
And with good harte, allow this our accion."
[Reprint Apoph. Erasmus, by Mr. Robert Roberts, Boston.]

† In Jonson's Christmas his Masque as it was presented at Court 1616, among the children is "Post and Paire. With a paire-Royall of Aces in his Hat; his Garment all done over with Payres and Purrs; his Squier carrying a Box, Cards and Counter." There is also "Wassall. Like a neat Sempster or Songster; her Page bearing a browne bowle drest with Ribbands and Rosemarie before her."

Pricket, i. 24.
Prick-madam, ii. 17.
Prince, ii. 62.
Primme, iii. 94.
Produce, iii. 207.
Profuser, ii. 226.
Progermination, ii. 251.
Propulsive, ii. 111.
Proscenium, ii. 57.
Prospective, ii. 220.
Protestant, ii. 6.
Prove, i. 109.
Protonotarie, iii. 145.
Prove, i. 109.
Ptsick, ii. 50.
Purfling, ii. 173.
Purls, ii. 136, 235.
Purslain, iii. 137.
Push, of pikes, iii. 170.
Push-pin, i. 29 : ii. 223.
Pushes, ii. 182.
Put = pusht, i. 29.
Pyramides, i. 147.

Q.

Quarelets, i. 41.
Quarter-acts, iii. 210.
Quick, ii. 140.
Quintell, ii. 93, 214 : iii. 41.
Quorum, iii. 36

R.

Rag'd, iii. 205.
Raile, ii. 74.
Reaching, ii. 13.
Reaks, i. 96.
Reaming, iii. 176.
Reconverse, iii. 33.
Recollect, ii. 239.
Recure, iii. 62.
Recommit, iii. 214.
Rector, ii. 41.
Rectresse, iii. 73.
Redeem, ii. 105.
Regredience, ii. 210.
Regression, ii. 252.
Reiterate, iii. 56.
Religious, i. 14.
Re-meeting, ii. 61.
Remora, i. 24.
Rents, ii. 133.
Reeve, ii. 74.
Repullulate, ii. 48.
Repullulation, ii. 273.
Repleat, ii. 128.
Repurgation, ii. 144.
Residenciarie, ii. 206.
Resident, ii. 149.
Resigne, i. 125.
Respasses, ii. 70.
Retorted, i. 139.

Retract, ii. 75.
Revolve, ii. 274.
Ribanings, iii. 40.
Rids, iii. 139.
Rifts, iii. 60.
Ropes, ii. 217.
Round, i. 12 : ii. 9, 161, 214 : iii. 165.
Roundelay, ii. 94.
Rosemarie, ii. 217.
Rowle=roll, iii. 21.
Rubelet, ii. 208.
Ruffe, ii. 74.

S.

Sack, i. 132.
Sack posset, ii. 19.
Sacietie, iii, 25.
Sad, ii. 287.
Sagge, ii. 25-6.†
Salt, i. 134, ii. 245.
Saints-bells, ii. 262.
Salute, iii. 183.
Salvages, i. 48 : ii. 10.
Sampler, i. 17, 180.
Saturitie, iii. 184.
Say, iii. 20, 29.
Say, and hold, iii. 181.
Scar-fire, i. 35 : ii. 28.
Scarre-crów-like, ii. 222.
Sceanes, i. 132 : ii. 253 : iii. 27.
Scene, ii. 244.
Schisme, ii. 131.
Sciography, ii. 59.
Scrip, i. 123 : ii. 116.
Scores, iii. 75, 166.
Sea-horse, i. 51.
Seldome, i. 64.
Sement, ii. 193.
Sere, i. 101.
Servility, iii. 2.
Severe, ii. 263.
Shagg'd, i. 76.

† The following are apposite examples of this word in Nash's *Pierce Pennilesse* :—" vpstarts that out-face towne and countrey in their veluets when Sir Rowland Russet-coat, their dad, goes *sagging* euerie day in his round gascoynes of white cotton, and hath much adoe (poore pennie-falter) to keep his vnthrift elbowes in reparation " (p. 8). " At length (as Fortune serude) I lighted vppon an old straddling usurer, clad in a damaske cassocke, edged with fox-furre; a pair of trunke slops, *sagging* down like a shoomaker's wallet," &c., (p. 11). (See under fox-furre in this Index.)

Shamefact'nesse, iii. 8.
Sharp-fang'd, ii. 175.
Shelfe, ii. 123.
Sheparling, ii. 151.
Shephardling, i. 9.
Shey, iii. 100.
Shewers, ii. 14.
Shor'd, i. 67.
Shore, ii. 166 : ii. 35.
Shots, i. 21 : ii. 119.
Shoulders, ii. 64.*
Sheering-feast, ii. 214.
Sick-of-love, ii. 92.
Silke-soft, ii. 76.
Silver-footed, iii. 56.
Silver-shedding, i. 86 : ii. 150.
Silver-wristed, iii. 57.
Simnel, ii. 224.
Simplicities, ii. 55.

Simper, i. 127.
Simpring, i. 57 : ii. 151.
Sincere, i. 102, 107 : ii. 67, iii. 181.
Sinceritie, i. 19 : ii. 243.
Sir John, ii. 178.
Size, i. 63.
Skurfe, iii. 216.
Slam, ii. 228.
Slave, i. 173.
Slit, ii. 51.
Sleued, iii. 94.
Slug-a-bed, i. 116.
Sluttish, ii. 253.
Smallage, i. 46, 155.
Smell-feast, iii. 22.
Smirk, i. 74.
Smirking, i. 177.
Smooth-pac't, ii. 255.
Smooth-skin, ii. 151.

* " Near House of Law by *Temple*-Bar,
Now man of Mace cares not how far,
In stockings Blew he marcheth on,
With Velvet Cape his Cloack upon ;
In Girdle, Scrowles, where names of some,
Are written down' whom touch of Thumbe
On Shoulder left must safe convoy,
Anoying Wights with name of Roy.
Poor Pris'ners friend that sees the touch,
Cries out, aloud, I thought as much."
     Davenant, p. 291.

Smutch, ii. 176.
Snugging, i. 42.
Sociate, iii. 8.
Sodden, iii. 23.
Sodders, iii. 23.
Soiles, iii. 137.
Sold, ii. 250.
Sometimes, ii. 105.
Souce, ii. 202, 269.
Soundlesse, iii. 173.
Soyl'd, ii. 213.
Spell, ii. 262.
Sperrables, ii. 207.
Speares, iii. 120.
Sphere, iii. 164.
Sphering=revolving, ii. 54.
Spinners, ii. 103, 109.
Sports, i. 10.
Sporting, i. 60.
Spring, i. 14.
Springall, i. 25.
Square, i. 62.
Stamp, i. 100.
Staffe, i. 124.
Starre-led, ii. 187.*
State, i. 13, ii. 280.
Staited, ii. 153.

State-like, i. 38.
St.=Saints, i. 157.
Stay, iii. 99.
Stench, ii. 285.
Steem, iii. 97.
Steerling, ii. 237.
Steletto, i. 30.
Still, ii. 122.
Stint, i. 58.
Stinted, iii. 103.
Stocks, ii. 129.
Stool-ball, ii. 226.
Stones, ii. 245.
Storax, ii. 45, 90.
Streakes, ii. 37.
Stringlesse, iii. 148.
Strutt, ii. 219.
Strutting, ii. 25-6, 219.
Suger'd, ii. 236.
Summer-birds, ii. 80.
Summer-friends, ii. 80.
Sunck, ii. 109.
Superlast, ii. 87.
Supervive, ii. 163.
Supraentitie, iii. 121.
Swadling-clout, iii. 144.
Sweating-closet, ii. 76.

* The pseudo-phenomenon was earlier and later employed by the Royalists to glorify "our most religious King," especially at the "glorious" Restoration.

GLOSSARIAL INDEX.

Sweet, i. 93.
Sweets, ii. 57.
Sweet-breath, ii. 61.
Sweetling, ii. 198.
Sweet-sad, ii. 94.
Swerved, i. 44.
Swinger, iii. 59.
Sybells, ii. 234.

T.

Tabbies, ii. 176, iii. 144.
Tally, iii. 166.
Tanner, farting, ii. 86.*
Tansie, ii. 227.
Tardidation, iii. 184.
Teases, ii. 287.
Tearmly, iii. 35.
Teaster, ii. 84.
Tearce, iii. 15.
Tearcely, i. 59.
Tedious, ii. 23.
Telling, ii. 16.
Teemd, i. 181.

Teen, ii. 271.
Teend, iii. 6.
Teending, ii. 269.
Τελοσ, iii. 224.
Temper, ii. 78 : iii. 11.
Tent, i. 30.
Ternarie, ii. 246.
Terce, i. 140.
Tettar, iii. 208
The, ii. 293
Theeving = slipping away, iii. 207
Then = than, i. 19, and throughout
There, iii. 103
Threshold, i. 95
Thumb, i. 50, 60 : ii. 198
Thumblesse, iii. 48
Thyrse, i. 12 : ii. 160
Thrumme, i. 132
Thronclet, ii. 281
Tiffanie, i. 13, 56 : ii. 18
Till, iii. 102

* There was a Tanner whose unsavory exploits have been variously chronicled. He appears to have beaten the Miller of Mansfield, of Percy's Reliques' ballad, in the vigour of his 'cracks,' and to have immortalized himself by letting-fly point-blank in the king's face as he was giving him a leg up on his horse. This and much more will be found in "King Edward II. and the Tanner of Tamworth." Shirley in his " Fairies " remembers " The men of ginger-bread."

Tincture, i. 19, 129 : iii. 171
Tingles, iii. 79
Tinseld, ii. 105
Tinselling, i. 57 : ii. 173
Title, ii. 236
Tittyries, ii. 36
Toadstones, ii. 107*
Tods, ii. 260
Tonguelesse, i. 100.
Toning, ii. 113.
Too, ii. 88 : iii. 99, 104.
Too-too, ii. 144.
Took, i. 21.
Topick, ii. 116.
Top-gallant, ii. 168.
Toucht, ii. 223.
Trammell net, ii. 214.
Trammelets, iii. 92.
Tramplers, ii. 31.
Trasy, ii. 241 : iii. 33.
Trebius, ii. 74.
Trencher-creature, ii. 73.
Trentall, i. 154: ii. 179, 211, 225 : iii. 37.
Troule, ii. 221.
True-love-knots, ii. 112.
Tucker, ii. 182.
True, iii. 133.

True-pac'd, ii. 77.
Truss, iii. 33.
Turne-broach, iii. 82.
Turbant, i. 163.
Turfe, i. 137.
Twelfth-tide King, iii. 166.
Twilight, ii. 295 : iii. 62.
Two, ii. 20.

U.

Umber, i. 65.
Unrude, ii. 72.
Unsluce, i. 24.
Unshorne, i. 116 : ii. 300.
Unchipt, iii. 136.
Unflead, iii. 136.
Unhallowed, iii. 119.
Under-dead, i. 180.
Under-lies, i. 180.
Underpropt, iii. 35.
Unperplext, ii. 187.
Unsmooth, ii. 171 : iii. 184.
Unsober, ii. 181.
Unsoft, ii. 251.
Uptailes, ii. 242.
Untruths, ii. 303.
Use, iii. 106.

* By a singular blunder the foot-note here is = infants. On 'Toadstones' see Bailey s. v.

V.

Vaile, yellow, i. 94.
Valentine, i. 52-3, 96.
Veales, ii. 74 : iii. 204.
Velome, ii. 110.
Venter, ii. 186.
Vestiments, iii. 34, 50.
Vesterie, i. 161 : ii. 91.
Vigil, ii. 71.
Vineger, ii. 298.
Virtue, ii. 16, 76.
Vizard, ii. 73.
Vultures, ii. 296.

W.

Wafer, ii. 59.
Wakes, i. 7 : ii. 256.
Warden, ii. 70.
Waste, i. 68 : ii. 86.
Watched, i. 160 : ii. 20.
Warpt, ii. 71.
Washt, or's, ii. 51.
Wassaile, i. 7 : ii. 271.*
Wassell boule, ii. 37.
Wassailing, ii. 271.
Weary, i. 101.
Weare, iii. 102.
Were, ii. 114.

Weed, ii. 30.
Weres, ii. 85.
We'l, ii. 105.
Weekly-strewings, i. 15.
Wheales, ii. 287.
Whelk, ii. 287.
Whimpering, ii. 130.
Whipping-cheere, iii. 173, 219.
Whorry, ii. 91.
Whit-flaw, i. 113 : ii. 107.
White, i. 42 : ii. 86, 114, 139, 158, 162, 255 : iii. 103, 223.
Wimbling, ii. 302.
Wood, corrupted, ii. 107.
Wool, whitest, i. 99, 149.
Woolie-bubbles, ii. 108.
Wort, ii. 164 : iii. 65, 137.
Woosted, iii. 176.
Wrapt, i. 23.
Wrie-nosed, ii. 171.
Writhing, i. 28.

Y.

Yerk, iii. 63.
Yirkt, ii. 72.
Yet, ii. 222.
Yonker, i. 111.

---

* See note in this Glossarial-Index under 'Post and Paire.'

Younglings, ii. 71, 201.
You, ii. 72.

Z.

Zeallesse, ii. 294.
Zonulet, i. 68.

INDEX OF NAMES.

In order not to over-burden the Glossarial-Index, the proper names—persons, and a few places—are given here by themselves. Under several will be found supplementary information overlooked in the Memorial-Introduction and Essay—because promised in foot-notes.

A.

Abdie, Lady, ii. 69.
Absyrtus, iii. 29.
Alablaster, Dr., ii. 258.
A-Lapide, iii. 197.
Ambrose, St., iii. 196, 197, 213.
Anthea, i. 19, 34, 40, 56: ii. 7, 223, 267, 294: iii. 49, 64.
Anacreon, i. 43, 67, 84, 167: iii. 21.
Apollo, i. 116: ii. 29, 81, 300 *et passim.*
Aquinas, iii. 191.
Aristophanes, iii. 80.
Aristotle, i. 62: ii. 296: iii. 85.
Augustine, St., iii. 186, 197, 210, 212.

B.

Bacon, ii. 101.
Bacchus, i, 12, 28, 67, 140: ii. 30, 38, 91, 263 *et passim.*
Bailey, i. 7, 24, 65, 161.
Baldwin, Prudence, ii, 29, 80, 268.
Barnfield, i. 8.
Bartly, ii. 216.
Basil, St., iii. 199.
Batt, i. 123.
Beanes, Parson, ii. 101.
Becon, i. 23.
Benlowes, i. 70.
Berkley, Sir John, ii. 250.
Bernard, St., iii. 195.
Bernard of Toledo, iii. 195.

INDEX OF NAMES.

Bethlehem, i. 149.*
Biancha, i. 49, 54 : iii. 6, 43.
Bice, ii. 273.
Blanch, i. 55 : ii. 172.
Blinks, ii. 287.
Blisse, iii. 22.
Boëtius, iii. 190.
Bold, Henry (H. B.), i. 52.
Boreman, iii. 55.
Bran, ii. 196.
Brand, i. 14, 15, 34, 53.
Bradshaw, Mrs. Katherine, i. 163.
Braithwaite, ii. 265.
Bridgeman, i. 65.
Bridget, ii. 92.
Brock, ii. 9.
Broomsted, ii. 165.
Brugel, ii. 79.
Brutus, i. 10.
Buckingham, i. 173.
Buggins, iii. 50.
Bunce, i. 144.
Bungie, ii. 30.
Burns, i. 66 : iii. 35.
Burr, iii. 22.
Byron, i. 51.

C.
Carew, ii. 3.
Carlile, Countess of, i. 110.
Cartwright, William, iii. 88.
Cassius, Iatrosophista, or Cassius Felix, i. 135.
Cassiodorus, iii. 185, 190.
Cato, i. 10.
Catullus, i. 40, 49, 86, 94, 97, 119, 124, 140, 141, 164 : ii. 253, 291 : iii. 13.
Center, ii. 85.
Chapman, i. 161.
Charles I, i. 41, 43, 105 : ii. 4, 93, 224, 283 : iii. 30, 124, 159, 161, 165.
Charles, Prince of Wales (= Charles II.), i. 5, 148 : ii. 187, 254.
Chaucer, i. 53.
Chipperfield, ii. 86.
Chub, iii. 75.
Churton, i. 23.
Cicero, ii. 232 : iii. 58, 105.
Cleopatra, ii. 231, 281.
Clunn, iii. 21.
Cob, ii. 207.

* The 'star' that appeared on the birthday of our "most religious king," Charles II., shines in all the contemporary verse and on The Restoration ('glorious!') it reappears with shocking fulsomeness.

INDEX OF NAMES.

Cock, ii. 187.
Comely, ii. 275.
Coone, ii. 181.*
Corinna, i. 81, 116, 168.†
Coryat, ii. 115.
Cotgrave, i. 8, 132 : ii. 70.
Cotta, i. 70.
Cotton, iii. 24.
Coxu, ii. 79.
Cowper, iii. 171.
Crab, ii. 218.
Crashaw, i. 68 : ii, 26, iii. 90.
Craw, ii. 99.
Crew, Sir Clipseby and Lady, ii. 12, 98, 134, 146, 160, 192 : iii. 37.‡
Crofts, ii. 276.
Croot, iii. 82.
Cuffe, i. 66.
Cunctatus, ii. 250.
Cupid, i. 108 : iii. 21, 84 *et passim*.
Cuts, ii. 68.

D.

Daniel, Samuel, i. 100.
Damescene, iii. 188.
Dardanus, i. 50.
Davies, Sir John, ii. 151.
Davies of Hereford, ii. 115.
Dean-Bourn, i. 48.
Deb, iii. 82.
Demophon, ii. 189.
Demosthenes, iii. 105.
Denham, ii. 220.
Diana, i. 86.
Dianeme, i. 56, 105 : ii. 85, 157, 224, 285.
Dibdin, i. 103.
Diodorus, ii. 174.
Dionysius, i. 28.
Distaff, St., iii. 55.
Dodsley, ii. 265.
Doll, ii. 77 : iii. 72.
Donne, ii. 50, 217, 291
Dorchester, Marquesse of, iii. 31.

* Simon Cowne and Edward, Richard and Lawrence occur in the Dean Prior register—same as Coone.

† Did Randolph in his " Complaint against Cupid, that he never made him in love," intend Herrick in these lines ?

"This on his Cloris spends his thoughts and time ;
That chaunts Corinna in his amorous rhyme."

‡ In II. 98 the passing quarrel may be compared with Herrick's words to the Bp. of Lincoln. He was placable and genial.

INDEX OF NAMES.

Dorset, Earl of, ii. 143.
Drayton, ii. 265.
Dryden, i. 47.
Dundrige, ii. 155.*

E.

Ecles, ii. 84.
Electra, i. 34, 57, 100: ii. 86, 156, 170, 215, 251, 260, 287, 301.
Exeter, Bishop of, i. 109.†

F.

Fabius, i. 70.
Falconbridge, Mrs. Margaret, ii. 272.
Falconbrige, Thomas, ii. 132.
Faunus, iii. 41.
Finch, iii. 28.
Fish, Sir Edward, ii. 82.
Fletcher, Giles, ii. 176.
Fletcher, John, iii. 109.
Flimsey, ii. 97.
Flood, iii. 83.
Florio, ii. 76.
Fone, ii. 66.
Ford, ii. 26.
Franck, ii. 177, 243.
Fuller, Thomas, iii. 21.
Fuller Worthies' Library, i. 8, 55: ii. 26, 291.

G.

Gander, ii. 201.
George-a-Green, ii. 264.
George the Pinner, ii. 265.
Gifford, Humph., i. 128.
Giles, Sir Edward and Lady, iii. 113.
Glasco, i. 78.
Glasse, ii. 80.
Gough, iii. 151.
Gorgonius, iii. 68.
Gotiere, i. 67.
Gryll, i. 82.
Groynes, ii. 2.
Greedy, ii. 42.
Grudgings, ii. 196.
Grubs, iii. 72.

* Dundridges occur frequently in the Dean Prior register. Marie, the d. of Christopher Dundridge, was buried the 9th of October, 1643, and Christopher, sonne of John Dundridge, the 18th of January, 1643.

† The 'Satires' of Hall and other Poems could not but form a bond of union with Herrick.

Gubbs, i. 138.
Guesse, i. 171.
Gut, iii. 75.

H.

Hall, John, i. 116: iii. 27.
Halliwell, ii. 36, 189: iii. 42, 53, 136.
Hanch, ii. 290.
Harmar, iii. 32.
Hastings, Lord, iii. 110.
Hazlitt, W. C., i. 34, 49: iii. 90.
Heale, Sir Thomas, ii. 298.
Heath, Robert, i. 154.
Heidelberg, ii. 115.
Herbert, George, i. 8: ii. 77, 80: iii. 76, 157, 219.
Hercules, i. 136.
Herrick, Bridget, ii. 169.
Herrick, Elizabeth, i. 39: ii. 70.
Herrick, Julia, iii. 57.
Herrick, Mercie, ii. 280.
Herrick, Nephew, ii. 79.*
Herrick, Nicholas (father), i. 45.
Herrick, Nicholas, jun., iii. 80.
Herrick, Robin, i. 32, iii. 14.
Herrick, Susannah, ii. 152: iii. 37.
Herrick, Thomas, i. 57: iii. 39.
Herrick, William, i. 125.
Hesiod, ii. 279: iii. 117.
Hog, iii. 72.
Holbein, ii. 79.
Homer, i. 86, 139: ii. 52, 91.
Hooker, iii. 16.
Hopton, Lord, iii. 47.
Horace, i. 53, 61, 67, 109, 120, 121, 158: ii. 39, 41, 47, 48, 50, 66, 81, 91, 104, 110, 118, 132, 188, 242, 243, 269, 300: iii. 14, 42, 49, 64, 68, 88, 149.
Horne, ii. 183.
Hymen, i. 90, *et frequenter*.

I.

Iphis S*t*., ii. 113.
Iphyclus, i. 135.
Irene, ii. 170
Isis, i. 135.
Ixion, i. 59.

---

* No trace remains of the 'painter' Herrick.

J.

Jack and Jill, ii. 101, 141.
James II., i. 5.
Jerome St., iii. 212.
Jincks, ii. 295.
Jocasta, i. 80.
Johnson Dr., iii. 17.
Jollie, i. 107.
Jolley and Jilly, ii. 88.
Jone, ii. 155, 211.
Jonson, i. 47, 92, 93, 99, 127: ii. 12, 14, 78, 126, 127, 185: iii. 11.
Jove, i. 101, *et passim*.
Judith, ii. 62.
Julia, i. 12, 13, 19, 21, 24, 32, 35, 37, 50, 68, 69, 102, 112, 114, 119, 122, 142, 168: ii. 27, 40, 42, 57, 59, 90, 102, 103, 110, 141, 158, 168, 179, 191, 195, 238, 247, 249, 250, 267, 283, 294, 295, 299, 303: iii. 7. 20, 28, 36, 70, 76, 78.
Juvenal, ii. 235.

K.

Keats, i. 38.
Kellam, iii. 14.
Kemble, ii. 51.
Keneday, Mrs. Dorothy, i. 72.*

L.

Laniere, i. 148: ii. 293.
Lawes, Henry and William, ii. 293: iii. 10, 160, 162.
Leander, i. 71.
Leo, i. 8.
Lentullus, i. 70.
Lesbia, i. 181.
Leech, ii. 34.
Leominster, ii. 105.
Letcher, ii. 155.
Lee (see Tracie.)
Lillie, i. 74.
Lincoln, Bp. of, i. 88: iii. 106.
Linnit, ii. 78.
Linus, ii. 174.
Loach, ii. 280.
Lovelace, ii. 123.
Lowman, Mrs. Bridget, ii. 60.
Lucia, ii. 184, 226, 243, 244: iii. 35.
Lucie, ii. 207.
Lucretius, iii. 25.
Lulls, ii. 2.

* Further research has failed to shed light on the 'fair lady's' history. I have an impression that she is elsewhere celebrated.

INDEX OF NAMES.

Lungs, ii. 201.
Lupes, iii. 34.
Luske, iii. 83.
Lydgate, i. 53.
Lyly, i. 180.

M.

Mab, ii. 202.
Maria (queen), i. 43 : ii. 5, 187.
Martial, i. 65, 78 : ii. 140, 291 : iii. 33.
Mars, ii. 80.
Magot, ii. 149.
Massinger, ii. 2.
Marvell, i. 8.
Mease, ii. 64.
Megg, iii. 23.
Menes, Sir Matthew, i. 91.
Merrifield, i. 156.
Mickle, i. 111.
Milton, i. 16, 38, 47, 116 : ii. 16, 28, 176, 202, 249, 280 : iii. 90.
Minerva, ii. 155.
Michelditch, ii. 275.

Moore (=Little), i. 24.
Moon, ii. 66.
Montaigne, ii. 76.
Momus, ii. 211.
Muchmore, i. 127.
Mudge, iii. 32.*
Myntz (=Mennes), ii. 154.†
Myrrha, i. 80.

N.

Nares, i. 159 : iii. 151.
Neptune, ii. 41.
Newark, ii. 194.
Nicot, i. 23.
Nicholson, ii. 15.
Nis, iii. 6.
Nodes, ii. 282.
Norgate, Edward, ii. 29.
Northly, Henry, ii. 33.
Nott, Dr., i. 8, 23, 26, 52, 53, 67, 89, 92, 94, 97, 110, 116, 119, 122, 124, 141, 164 : ii. 242, 265, 291 : iii. 4, 5, 13, 35, 55, 88.
Nowell, Dean, i. 23.

* Robert, Bartholomew and Richard Mudge, are in the Dean Prior Register—a common Devonshire name.

† Doubtless Herrick became acquainted with this Knight through his contributions to " Wit's Recreations," fully noticed in Memorial-Introduction.

O.

Oberon, ii. 24, 104, 203, *et passim*.
Oenone, ii. 111, 272, 286.
Oulsworth, iii. 77.
Origen, iii. 197, 212.
Orpheus, ii. 274.
Ovid, i. 17, 26, 89, 139 : ii. 189, 295, 300 : iii. 25.

P.

Pagget, i. 111.
Panchaia, i. 98 : iii. 222.
Parson, Sir Thomas, i. 160.
Parsons, Mrs. Dorothy, ii. 141.
Parsons, T'omasin iii. 38.
Parrat, ii. 141.
Parrie, Sir George, iii. 66.
Paske, ii. 64.
Pastillos, iii. 68
Patrick, ii. 92.
Paul, ii. 245.
Pclops, i. 59.
Peapes, ii. 287.
Pearch, ii. 276.
Peason, ii. 290.

Pemberton, Sir Lewis, ii. 71.
Pembroke, Earl of, ii. 62.
Pennie, iii. 45.
Perenna, i. 16, 155, 179 : ii. 125 : iii. 37, 74.
Perilla i. 14, 101 : iii. 53.
Persius, i. 97 : ii. 51, 253, 291.
Petrarch, i. 8.
Phillis, ii. 112, 150, 189.
Pink, ii. 8.
Pievish, ii. 88.
Pimple, iii. 83.
Pliny, ii. 118.
Plato, ii. 148, 248 : iii. 58.
Pope, iii. 66, 156.
Porter, Endymion, i. 70, 124, ii. 136, 212 : iii. 70.*
Pot, i. 165.
Potter, Bp. of Carlisle, ii. 33.*
Potter, Mrs. Grace, iii. 43.
Porter, Amie, ii. 288.
Portman, Mrs., iii. 73.
Prat, ii. 227.
Prew, ii. 80, 268.
Prigg, i. 123 : ii. 66.
Prickles, iii. 9.

* Notices of Porter will be found in Mr. Huth's "Inedited Poetical Miscellanies" 1870. Notes, sig. Ff. Randolph's "Pareneticon" to him is finely touched.

Propertius, i. 104, 140.
Punchin, ii. 286.
Pusse, ii. 265.
Pythagoras i. 104, 140.

R.

Radcliffe, Sir George, i. 23.
Ralph, ii. 62 : iii. 29.
Ramsey, i. 120.
Randolph, ii. 170 : iii. 76.
Raspe, ii. 84.
Reape, ii. 303.
Reynolds, iii. 17.
Richmond, and Lennox, Duke of, ii. 113.*
Rook, ii. 102.
Roots, ii. 99.
Ruben, ii. 79.
Rumpe, iii. 82.
Rush, Robin, ii. 86 : iii. 84.

S.

Sallust, ii. 100.
Sappha, ii. 249.
Sapho, i. 70 : ii. 64, 227, 276, 298 : iii. 41.
Saints (Jesting names of), i. 158.
Scobble, i. 75.
Secundus, i. 49, 122.
Selden, John, ii. 65 : iii. 35.
Shakspeare, i. 7, 26, 32, 63, 99, 128, 133, 174, 179 : ii. 51, 93, 118, 129, 173, 210, 236, 241, 298, 303.
Shapcott, ii. 110.†
Shark, ii. 24.
Shift, ii. 68.
Shewbread, ii. 97.
Shopter, iii. 82.
Sidney, i. 55, 100, 180 : ii. 94, 236.
Simonides, i. 62, 71.
Sibilla, ii. 168.
Silvia, i. 13, 36 : ii. 172, 208 : iii. 10, 19.

* The " three brave brothers " celebrated, were—
 (1) George Stuart, Lord D'Aubigny, slain at Edgehill 23 Oct., 1642.
 (2) Lord John Stuart, killed at the battle of Alresford in 1644.
 (3) Lord Bernard Stuart, who fell at Rowton Heath in 1655. They were sons of Esme, 3d duke of Lennox.

† Further research has not elicited more on this name. Could it be a character-name?

INDEX OF NAMES.

Sibb, ii. 246.
Skelton, i. 180.
Skoles, ii. 207.
Skurfe, ii. 131.
Skinns, ii. 88.
Skrew, ii. 78.
Slouch, ii. 254.
Smeaton, ii. 230.
Sneape, ii. 32.
Snare, ii. 196.
Southwell, Robert, ii. 238.
Southwell, Susannah, ii. 153.
Southwell, Sir Thomas and Lady, i. 90.
Soame, Anne, ii. 69.
Soame, Stephen, ii. 162.
Soame, Sir Thomas, ii. 124.
Soame, Sir William, ii. 45.
Sophocles, ii. 237.

Spalt, ii. 182.
Spenser, i. 181 : iii. 134.
Spelman, ii. 77.
Spenke, iii. 1.
Spokes, iii. 38.
Spur, iii. 79.
Stowe, i. 116.
Stuart, Bernard Lord, i. 108. 154.
Strut, i. 90.
Strutt, i. 172 : ii. 37 : iii. 4.
Strada, iii. 26.
Stewart, Sir Simeon, ii. 36.
Stanes, i., 72.
Stanley, Thomas, ii. 95.*
Steevens, iii. 265.
Stone, Mary, ii. 259.
Stone, Sir Richard, ii. 139.†
Suckling, ii. 153.

* The poem here promised is as follows:—
"Those oaks that most obdurate are,
　Shall willingly their arms unwind;
And by themselves engraven, wear
　My verse upon their Leaves, and Rind:
And every Tree, whose Top prefers
To Heaven these sacred Characters,
　No storms shall offer to invade.
For whilst thus charm'd, the rough Winds may
Hope with more ease, to snatch away
　Their fastned Roots, or fleeting shade."

† He was the only surviving son of John Stone, Sergeant at Law, brother of Mrs. Herrick, the poet's mother. He was Se-

INDEX OF NAMES.

Sudds, i. 170.
Swetnaham, iii. 76.

T.

Tanner, farting, ii. 86.
Tap, ii. 285.
Tennyson, i. 44, 62, 64, 93, 173 : ii. 20, 94, 95, 204, 302.
Thamasis, iii. 56.
Tibullus, i. 140.
Titian, ii. 79.
Tintoretto, ii. 79.
Topsell, ii. 234.
Tooly, ii. 171.
Tracie, Lady, ii. 191.
Trap, iii. 72.
Trapp, iii. 192.
Trasy, ii. 241 : iii. 33.
Tradescant, ii. 217.
Trencherman, ii. 274.
Trigg, ii. 230.
Truggin, ii. 304.
Trundell, Tim, ii. 87.

Tubbs, iii. 34.
Tuck, ii. 228.

U.

Umber, ii. 172.
Urbin, 79.
Ursley, ii. 159, 217.
Urles, ii. 177.

V.

Valentine, St., i. 52, 53, 96 : ii. 77.
Vandike, ii. 79.
Vaughan, Henry, ii. 136.
Venus, i. 95 : ii. 55, 58 : iii. 52, *et passim*.
Villars, Lady Mary, ii. 56.*
Vineger, iii. 32.
Virgil, i. 77, 97, 135, 181 : ii. 237, 274 : iii. 49, 79.
Vulcan, ii. 188.

W.

Warr, i. 81 : ii. 166.†

condary of Wood Street Compter in London. He died 20th September, 1660.

   * This was a Villiers ; and her Letters abound—showing all the family capacity and eke their strange spelling even for the period.

   † Randolph has an "Epitaph upon his honoured Friend, Master Warre." It begins :—

     "Here lies the knowing head, the honest heart,

Weare, John, ii. 166.
Westminster, ii. 57 : iii. 56.
Westmoreland, i. 67, 175 : ii. 118, 194.
Wheeler, Mrs. Eliz., i. 79 : ii. 3 : iii. 69.
Wheeler, Mrs. Penelope, ii. 145.*
Wickes (=Weekes) ii. 47, 218 : iii. 65.
Willan, iii. 27.
Willand, Mrs. Mary, ii. 148.

Williams, (see *Lincoln*)
Williams, i. 8.
Wilson, i. 67: ii. 293.
Wingfield, ii. 181.

Y.

Yard, Lettice, ii. 33.†
Yorke, Duke of, ii. 5.

Z.

Zelot, ii. 217.

  Fair blood and courteous hands, and every part
   Of gentle Warre," &c.
Probably the same with Herrick's friend. Warre and Weare were also (I think) identical.

* I had hoped to give further details on the Wheelers; but nothing of any value has resulted from somewhat extensive inquiries. The Herricks and Wheelers were related by marriage.

‡ Barnabas Potter, Herrick's predecessor and appointed Bp. of Carlisle, married Elizabeth Yard, d. of Lady Giles by her first husband, and widow of Edward Yard (mother of the 'witty' Mrs. Lettice Yard), and it is probable therefore that he and his family continued to maintain rare intercourse with the parish. Hence our Poet's celebration of members of the Potter family. (For Potter see ii. 33.)

The Yardes at present hold the Giles Estates at Dean Prior. In our own day the name has been splendidly in honour.

FINIS.

ROBERT ROBERTS, PRINTER, BOSTON.

BINDING LIST JUL 15 1934

PR
3510
A5G76
1876
v.3

Herrick, Robert
    Complete poems

PLEASE DO NOT REMOVE
CARDS OR SLIPS FROM THIS POCKET

UNIVERSITY OF TORONTO LIBRARY

BIBLIOLIFE

Old Books Deserve a New Life
www.bibliolife.com

Did you know that you can get most of our titles in our trademark **EasyScript**™ print format? **EasyScript**™ provides readers with a larger than average typeface, for a reading experience that's easier on the eyes.

Did you know that we have an ever-growing collection of books in many languages?

Order online:
www.bibliolife.com/store

Or to exclusively browse our **EasyScript**™ collection:
www.bibliogrande.com

At BiblioLife, we aim to make knowledge more accessible by making thousands of titles available to you – quickly and affordably.

Contact us:
BiblioLife
PO Box 21206
Charleston, SC 29413